HOUSING WEALTH

3 Ways The New Reverse Mortgage is Changing Retirement Income Conversations

Part Of The Certified Housing Wealth Advisor
Curriculum™

DON GRAVES, RICP®

Foreword by Jamie Hopkins, CFP® and Tom Hegna, CHFC®

ISBN: 978-1-7320270-1-5

Amazon Paperback ISBN: 978-1-7320270-0-8

Interior Design: Christina Gorchos

DISCLAIMER

The views expressed in this book are those of the author and do not necessarily reflect the views of any institution or organization to which they are affiliated.

This material has been prepared for informational purposes only and should not be relied on for tax, legal, or accounting advice.

You should consult with an attorney or other professional to determine what may be best for your client's individual needs.

TABLE OF CONTENTS

ABOUT DON GRAVES

D on Graves, RICP®, is one of the nation's leading edu-cators on reverse mortgages in retirement income planning. He is the president of the Housing Wealth Institute and is an adjunct professor of retirement income at The American College of Financial Services. He was the first reverse mortgage professional to obtain the coveted Retirement Income Certified Professional (RICP®) desig-nation from The American College.

Over the past two decades, Don has developed a knack for common-sense analysis and advanced reverse mortgage application. The American College course Don is featured in currently has more than 16,000 advisors enrolled. His personal practice has generated more than 12,000 con-sultations, leading to nearly 3,000 clients.

As both an educator and skilled practitioner, Don has a unique perspective that very few share. His RICP® designation equips him to understand the unique retirement planning needs and concerns that consumers have, along with their hesitation when it comes to reverse mortgages.

Don has been quoted in *Forbes* magazine and featured on PBS-sponsored shows as well as other venues and programming. He is a sought-after professional speaker and served as a guest member on the Funding Longevity Task Force (now part of The American College). This group was instrumental in providing the research that led to the Financial Industry Regulatory Authority (FINRA) reversing its long-standing position on reverse mortgages.

He holds an undergraduate degree in finance from Temple University, as well as graduate studies in economics at Eastern University. Don resides in Greater Philadelphia, is married, and has three children.

ACKNOWLEDGMENTS

I would first like to thank my Father, without whom none of this would exist. Thank you, Papa!

Thank you to my mother, Juanita Graves, who was the 1950 valedictorian of Oliver High School in Winchester, Kentucky. Though she was not able to afford college, she gave me the gift of education, wisdom, faith and courage. I am because of her sacrifice.

Thank you to my big sister, Michelle, who called me in 1999 when I was serving as president of Habitat for Humanity in Philadelphia. She said, "Little brother, you should consider reverse mortgages." I am grateful for Patty Wills, who hired me though I had no real experience, and Jim Mahoney for his pioneering leadership in the reverse mortgage space. I am also thankful for my first mentor and dear friend, the late Monte Rose, whose input in my business life was valuable beyond measure.

I am appreciative of Torrey Larsen for his passionate and principled leadership within the reverse mortgage industry and for his foresight to champion the formation of the Funding Longevity Task Force. Torrey has given me space and support to grow ideas and expand boundaries; his friendship is precious. Thanks to the leadership team at Retirement Funding Solutions: Alex Pistone, Chris Kargacos, and Dan Shackelford. They are men of integrity and exemplify grace under pressure.

Many of the Task Force members have been instrumental in my development: Dr. Barry Sacks, Dr. Sandy Timmerman, Rita Cheng, Shelley Giordano, and Dr. Tom Davison. These folks received me as a colleague in the early days and helped to sharpen my knowledge and hone my skills. I am overwhelmed with gratitude for these relationships.

I was fortunate to meet Dr. Wade Pfau, who invited me to present at a lunch-and-learn event at The American College of Financial Services. This event was the catalyst for a series of life-changing introductions. Without Wade's help, I would not be where I am today.

I am profoundly grateful for David Littell. At our initial meeting, Dave served as the director of the RICP® program. He took great interest not only in reverse mortgages, but in me as a person. He facilitated my understanding of the concepts and principles of retirement income and gave me a platform to turn my experience into meaningful content for advisors across the country.

Out of that collaboration came an introduction to Jamie Hopkins, the current co-chair of the RICP® program. Jamie has become a great friend and encouragement to me. He has advocated on my behalf time and again and has opened many doors for me; I am glad to call him my brother.

Special thanks to Dr. C.W. Copeland, who helped me see beyond and pursue more.

Thanks to Curtis Cloke of THRIVE University and Retirement NextGen (RNG) software, who has become a close ally in championing housing wealth. He was gracious to introduce me to retirement income giant Tom Hegna, who shares in his presentations the power of using home equity wisely.

I was also introduced to the great folks at Ash Brokerage: Jim Ash, Tim Ash, and Mike McGlothlin. They have been energetic supporters of many initiatives in which I have been involved. Their friendship, partnership, and leadership have been fantastic.

I could not have completed this project without the help of Elise Chambers. Her work ethic and focus helped us get the job done.

Thanks to my best friend, Dr. Ron King. His friendship and wise counsel have kept me afloat time without measure.

Lastly and most significantly, I thank my wife of twenty-seven years, Shelle Graves. She has listened to my stories, dreamed with me, and wiped away the tears when things went sideways. She has been a devoted friend and true partner. I am blessed.

JAMIE HOPKINS FOREWORD

Holistic planning is the future of financial services. But at the same time, so is niche planning. So what does this mean? It means that financial planning needs to revolve around a coordinated team, that is looking out for the individual client's best interests. In doing so, home equity needs to be embraced as a potential retirement cash flow option. This brings us to reverse mortgages or the HECM. It is a name that is often met with hesitation or scorn. But the reality is that the product can help millions of Americans and most of the negative criticisms are misplaced due to a lack of knowledge.

As professor of retirement income planning at The American College of Financial Services, where I also serve as the co-director of the New York Life Center for Retirement Income Planning, I have attempted to keep an agnostic view of products when it comes to retirement income planning. But, to be honest, I also used to have a slightly negative and naive view of reverse mortgages. It was through my relationship with Don Graves, RICP® and president of the HECM Institute, that I began my journey to better understand reverse mortgages and how they fit into a comprehensive retirement income picture.

Over time, the information that I have learned from Don Graves has been invaluable. This information has helped me develop and shape the home equity portion of the RICP® designation program, impacting the way thousands of advisors view the topic. Don has a great grasp of how important home equity and reverse mortgages are to the retirement security of Americans.

Home equity is the single largest asset for American retirees. But, many advisors typically ignore the asset from a retirement income perspective. This is not prudent, it is not the best practice, and it does not give the client the best chance of achieving a successful retirement.

While reverse mortgages are not for every client, they can be a beneficial tool when used correctly. But, before you can utilize them correctly you need to understand how the product works and how it can support a client's retirement. The reality is that there isn't just one way to use a reverse mortgage, but many ways, just like there are many ways to use life insurance, investments, or an annuity.

I plead for financial advisors, financial service professionals, and American retirees to educate themselves on reverse mortgages and how they can be used to improve retirement security. Luckily for you, Don Graves knows reverse mortgages inside and out. He also knows how reverse mortgages fit into a retirement plan. As such, there is no better person than to learn more about reverse mortgages from than Don Graves.

Jamie Hopkins,
Esq., MBA, CFP, RICP

TOM HEGNA FOREWORD

As I write this foreword, I am flying at 35,000 feet from Gaunzhou, China to Singapore. From there, I will continue on to Bangkok, Thailand and speak to over 10,000 members of the Million Dollar Roundtable. I mention my travels because I get the opportunity to teach people around the world the *optimal* way to retire.

Notice I use the word "optimal" instead of "best" to describe retirement because no one knows what will be best. No one! The optimal solution simply means it will likely be the best solution more often than any other solution and it certainly won't be the worst.

On this premise, I have based my four books on retirement. My most recent book *Don't Worry, Retire Happy* was tied into my Public TV Special (that has now played in over 72 million homes in the U.S. and Canada). Step seven in that book is: "Use Your Home Equity Wisely." Now, I have to be honest. When I wrote that book, I had no idea there were so many ways to use home equity, or housing wealth as Don refers to it.

Don and I met, courtesy of our mutual friend, Curtis Cloke—speaker, author and software developer. Curtis holds a training class called "Thrive University," and it was at one of his courses that I met Don. Don had just given a short, 30-minute presentation on reverse mortgages, and it blew me away.

I was always a little skeptical of reverse mortgages because I saw them being sold by old, worn-out TV stars trying to make a buck off of retirement. But, what Don shared in that presentation and what he writes about in this book is entirely different from that. He shows you things you had no idea were even available to retirees, and it's all backed by the research of PhD's like Wade Pfau of the American College.

As an economist and author for over 25 years, I have witnessed the retirement challenges that Americans are facing. Overwhelmed baby boomers do not know where to turn for advice. Financial advisors are also facing a challenging journey with their clients as we move forward into an unknown economic future with new regulations.

Growing up in Glenwood, Minnesota, I was raised by my two parents who were school teachers, and both had pensions. When discussing retirement, they would talk in terms of "We are ready to retire since we have $3,000 a month in income." *Or* "With Social Security and our pension, we have enough income to last for the rest of our lives."

Fast forward to today's landscape and the conversation changes dramatically. Many people do not have a pension or an employee-sponsored retirement plan. Everyone is focused on obtaining a certain number, they just aren't sure how to get there.

In Chapter 11, Don references my first book, *Paychecks and Playchecks*. In that book, I share the importance of guaranteed lifetime income for a successful retirement; at a minimum, basic living expenses must be covered by this. Social Security and pensions count, but more often than not, there is a shortfall. I recommend covering any shortfall with a lifetime income annuity. Now, Don shows you that your clients' housing wealth can play an important role as well!

When you combine housing wealth with other retirement assets, a whole new dimension is added to what can be accomplished in retirement. Housing wealth can sustain income during a bear market when pulling money out of a portfolio could be disastrous. It can help delay Social Security benefits to age 70. It can serve as an emergency long-term care plan for people who cannot qualify for Long-Term Care Insurance. Don will show you many, many more examples of how housing wealth can increase retirement success and happiness.

Don's attention to detail makes this book a must read for financial advisors who want to improve their knowledge immediately. Don will take you deep into the world of housing wealth and reverse mortgages – what they are, how they work, what to take advantage of, what to be careful of, how the loans work, what type of investment strategies work best, the importance of self-discipline and so much more! Although this book may not solve every retirement problem, it is an ideal step forward.

Rather than leave retirement planning to chance, this book can provide real-world solutions to help you take action the moment you finish. I hope you enjoy Don's meticulous and practical retirement solutions as much as I have.

Tom Hegna
Economist, Author and Speaker
CLU, ChFC, CASL

INTRODUCTION

To say retirement planning has changed is perhaps the greatest understatement of this entire book. The advent of the baby boomers, the uncertainty of the current economic and political landscape, and the rise of a more sophisticated borrower all require a shift in planning.

Furthermore, the traditional tools and strategies available have not kept current with the changing times. Today's advisor has the herculean task of creating near-miraculous retirement outcomes in the face of less savings and longer life spans. They are called upon to be pilot, navigator, flight attendant, and baggage handler—ensuring a safe landing and enjoyable flight. It's not fair, but as a result of tremendous competition in the industry, it is expected.

The good news is that there is one resource giving "financial pilots" a completely new way to navigate the journey. This new tool is the newly restructured reverse mortgage.

Let's be honest; the reverse mortgage comes with "baggage" of its own. Historically, moderate to affluent retirees and their advisors have either dismissed the reverse mortgage as irrelevant (or even dangerous), or they have relegated it to a last-resort option.

However, much has changed. Recent research conducted by Nobel Prize winners, financial thought leaders, prestigious academic institutions, and scholarly journals now affirms the role that the strategic use of reverse mortgages can play in comprehensive retirement planning.

By no means am I suggesting a reverse mortgage is right for every client, but I do believe that the newly-restructured reverse mortgage is uniquely designed to address the most common concerns of retirement. Every advisor working with retirees must understand how it fits into the planning conversation.

You may have reservations. Most advisors do, but admittedly, something has changed. (Otherwise, you probably wouldn't be reading this book.)

Why Are a Growing Number of Advisors Embracing and Endorsing the Reverse Mortgage?

The answer is that they took a closer look. Perhaps it was something they read in a journal, heard in a conference, or learned in a class. Whatever it was, it piqued their interest (as it did yours) enough for them to explore it further.

Over the years, I've come across two types of advisors, and throughout this book, we will address the questions, concerns, and discoveries that these two types of advisors typically have. You'll find the advisors' journeys personified in the thoughts of Carol and Alvin; we think you will identify with them, especially through their advisor questions at the beginning of many of the chapters.

 **Carol:** Age fifty, CFP®, ChFC®, has been in the industry for twenty-three years. She and her team focus mainly on managed wealth with about 250 households.

Currently more than 70 percent of her clients are retiring or close to it. Most of them have saved well, but very few have a confidence level that they can weather the storms of a long retirement. She wants to learn about tools that can give her clients this type of confidence as well as protect them from premature asset erosion and attrition.

 Alvin: Age sixty-two, CLU® and RICP®, has been in the industry since he was twenty-three. He began with life and annuity sales and has primarily stayed in the genre. He has a steady six-figure income and remains MDRT qualified every year (top of the table most years).

Though he partners with other advisors to handle managed wealth, he primarily sees himself as a life/annuity specialist. He's helped thousands over the years and now wants to be able to have more significant planning conversations with his existing "transactional" clients in addition to learning ways to get in front of new ones.

Straightforward Talk to Help You See the Big Idea

In the title of this book, I mention that there are three specific ways reverse mortgages are shifting planning conversations. I want to share them now as you will find these themes repeated throughout the book. You will soon be able to identify them with ease.

1. Reverse mortgages have changed the way advisors **SEE** the housing asset.

2. Reverse mortgages have changed the way advisors **SOLVE** the five most pressing retirement concerns.

3. Reverse mortgages have changed the way advisors **SEAMLESSLY** incorporate housing wealth into planning.

As an advisor myself, I understand that your time is precious. Therefore, the concepts in this book are designed to be easily understood and immediately actionable, as well as:

- **Simplified**: As a professor of retirement income, I am not opposed to deep analytics. There are other books that do a great job with that. You will not find advanced, algorithmic calculus in this book. You will find straightforward, honest, back-of-the-napkin, kitchen table, common-sense conversations about reverse mortgages.

- **Insightful**: Once you understand what a reverse mortgage is and how it can be used, the lightbulb will come on. It's like test-driving a car, then seeing that model everywhere you go. Once you truly see the big idea, you will begin to see opportunities for its application everywhere you look.

- **Practical**: My goal for each section is to answer the pressing questions advisors have, help you identify the ideal clients for a particular strategy, give you precise verbiage to begin a conversation, and provide the tools to grow your practice.

Where to Begin?

This book is divided into four main sections.

+ **Section 1**: The Changing Retirement Income Landscape and How Housing Wealth is Shifting the Conversation » *Why Reverse Mortgages Are Important*

+ **Section 2**: Understanding the Newly Restructured Reverse Mortgage: What's New, What's Not, What's Hot » *What Reverse Mortgages Are*

+ **Section 3**: Case Studies and the Common Strategies Impacting Retirement Income Today » *When and Where Reverse Mortgages Should Be Used in Planning*

+ **Section 4**: Incorporating Home Equity into Your Practice » *How to Implement Reverse Mortgages into Your World*

Feel free to start at the beginning or jump to a chapter/section that captures your interest.

My Promise

I understand the stresses that come with finding new clients, serving and meeting the needs of existing clients, and making sure they don't erode assets prematurely or jump ship entirely. I know the intersection between logical planning and the behavioral dynamics of decision making. I recognize that your clients often have unreasonable expectations, and your personal livelihood and financial wellbeing are often inextricably tied to your performance. I understand your world. This book is written from that perspective—from one who has not only walked a mile in your shoes but worn your entire wardrobe!

Most advisors no longer have a completely negative picture of reverse mortgages. Many simply don't know where it fits in their practice, how to identify clients who may need it, how to broach the subject, how to communicate the concepts, or how to clarify its assimilation with other retirement income planning strategies. The goal of this book is to equip you to do those things.

I will make a bold promise: If you read this book with an open mind, by the time you finish, I guarantee you will have a better, deeper, richer understanding of what the reverse mortgage is, how it works, when it's appropriate for use and when it's not. In addition, you will also:

- Have the tools to allow you to lead more significant planning conversations with your existing clients and gain unprecedented access to new clients with investable resources.

- See how reverse mortgages can eliminate the most powerful risks to retirement income and identify new ways your clients can keep their assets working longer without having to sacrifice their lifestyle or enjoyment.

- Be able to demonstrate how reverse mortgages integrate with retirement income, investments, annuities, and insurances to create enhanced outcomes not otherwise achievable.

- Determine how suitable and appropriately placed insurance, annuities, and investments can be purchased without using the proceeds of the reverse mortgage.

SECTION 1:

THE CHANGING RETIREMENT INCOME LANDSCAPE

How Housing Wealth Is Shifting the Conversation

1

Discovering the Hidden Potential of Housing Wealth

I'm not opposed to reverse mortgages, but I think only a very small percentage of my clients would actually need one. How does this apply to me?

I keep hearing that reverse mortgages are different, but exactly how could the "new" reverse mortgages aid my clients?

How is home equity different from housing wealth?

Reverse mortgages are so controversial in the advising community, I'd rather not mention them at all. Are they worth the hassle?

Why are some advisors more successful than others? Is it good luck or being in the right place at the right time? Were some gifted at birth, while others worked hard and learned? Maybe they were successful because they saw something that others missed and took advantage of it. In many ways, this is what I think happened to Steve Jobs.

What the World's First Computer Mouse Has to Do with Your Success (or Lack Thereof)

In 1964, at the Stanford Research Institute in Menlo Park, California, computer scientist Douglas Engelbart stumbled onto something he thought could make a difference in the way people interacted with computers. He named his invention the X-Y Position Indicator for a Display System. Today, we know it as the computer mouse.

For the first time in history, you could control the computer without using key strokes or punch cards. His device didn't look like much, just a small, brown box a little larger than a person's hand, with a red button on top. But by using it, you could move the cursor on the screen, click on different icons, and "windows" would open.

In 1969, Engelbart demonstrated his new device for the leading computer experts. He had no takers. He showed technology giants IBM and Hewlett Packard, and they both said "no, thank you." Finally, Xerox's Palo Alto Research Center (PARC) said yes (as they did to most technological inventions), but even they failed to find a serious use for the device.

However, in late 1979, a 24-year-old entrepreneur, Steve Jobs, negotiated with Xerox to tour their PARC facility. What happened next is well documented. As Jobs was being shown various technology, he spotted the X-Y Position Indicator and asked to see what it did. Engineer Larry Tesler, who conducted the demonstration, later recounted his experience: "Jobs was pacing around the room, acting up the whole time. He was very excited . . . Then, when he began seeing the things I could do on-screen, he watched for about a minute and started jumping around the room, shouting, 'Why aren't you doing anything with this? This is the greatest thing. This is revolutionary!'"

The Xerox folks pressed Jobs to explain more of what he was seeing, but finally, he just said, "Never mind."

When Jobs left that day, he called a partner and told him that he found something that would change the world . . . and it did. Five years later, in 1984—twenty years after its invention—the X-Y Position Indicator for a Display System was redesigned and in-corporated into the Apple Macintosh as the world's first "mouse." To this day, it is still an indispensable part of our technology, from computers to tablets to phones and beyond.

How did the world's top computer scientists—IBM, Hewlett Packard, and Xerox—all miss it?

Perhaps a question once posed to Helen Keller can help. She was asked:

> *"Ms. Keller, is there anything worse than being blind?"*
>
> *She replied, "Yes, having sight and no vision."*

You see it, right? Xerox and the others had sight, but *Steve Jobs had vision.*

In the following chapters of this book, we will conduct a "demonstration" of the newly restructured HECM reverse mortgage. I am not sure you will reach Steve Jobs-level excitement—jumping up and down, hyperventilating, and shouting "This is revolutionary!"—but you may see something that others have missed. What you see could become an indispensable part of your practice, greatly benefit your clients, and differentiate you from other advisors. You may indeed have a "Steve Jobs moment" before it's all over!

Seven Outdated Reverse Mortgage Concerns

In early 2017, after speaking at a large conference for advisors and following up with a routine email, I received this surprising response:

> "{Company Name} is an independent, registered investment advisory firm managing nest eggs for over 400 client families. We have done extensive research on the reverse mortgage business and do not feel it is a prudent strategy for <u>any of our clients.</u>"

Though initially stunned by his written candor, I recognized his response as one of the seven concerns I've heard advisors express over the years. See if you can spot his below.

Reverse Mortgages Are:

- **Too Controversial:** "They have a lot of bad press, and it seems like when they do come up, the response is always negative ... I don't want my clients to look at me sideways if I mention them."

- **Too Complicated:** "They have too many bells, whistles, and hidden trap doors. I don't know anyone who understands them."

- **Too Expensive:** "I hear the costs are astronomical."

- **Equity Strippers**: "They don't leave any money to my clients' heirs."

- **Not Something My Clients Have Ever Asked About:** "I have never had a client actually ask me about them as something they would need."

- **Not for My Clients:** "Even if they did ask, my clients would never have a need for one."

- **Products That Should Only Be Used a Last Resort**: "I would only tell my clients to do one if they ran out of money and it was the last possible option."

Do these concerns sound familiar? My guess is that many of you reading this book once held or currently hold one or more of those opinions. Honestly, each of those concerns have an element of truth to them, though most are outdated, exaggerated, or misunderstood. Nevertheless, we will unpack all of them on our journey and share honest and straightforward answers to each.

The one good outcome concerning the advisor's email is that it caused me to rethink how I approach the topic. Now, I begin by asking advisors such as yourself to answer three simple questions, and my only request is that you answer honestly.

Three Simple Questions

 What percentage of your clients who are at or near retirement do you think would have a need for a reverse mortgage?

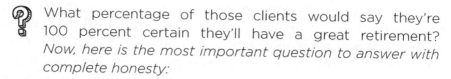 What percentage of those clients would say they're 100 percent certain they'll have a great retirement? *Now, here is the most important question to answer with complete honesty:*

If there were a proven resource that would allow those clients to increase cash flow, reduce retirement risks, preserve assets, improve liquidity, and add new dollars back into savings . . . what percentage of those clients would want you to tell them about it?

Did you answer 100 percent to the last question? Of course, you did. Most advisors do; truthfully, what advisor wouldn't?

Herein lies the disconnect. Advisors tend to answer that maybe 10–15 percent of their clients "might" have the need for a reverse mortgage and that only 10–15 percent of their clients are 100 percent certain they will have a great retirement.

They then acknowledge that 100 percent of those clients would want their advisor to tell them *what a reverse mortgage does!* That's right; those three things mentioned are the core building blocks of how the newly restructured reverse mortgage works. Surprise!

Why the huge gap between the typical perception of the reverse mortgage and the reality of what one accomplishes? I think I know the answer.

In 1997, I was president of Habitat for Humanity in Philadelphia. The board of directors provided me with my first cell phone. A cell phone! You couldn't tell me that I wasn't a first-round NFL draft choice, it was such a big deal. However, the phone only did two things: made and received phone calls, period!

Fast-forward twenty years to my son's "smart" phone. During the time he's had it, I have seen many texts sent, angry birds die, videos launch, snapchats come and go, and Facebook opinions posted, but the one thing I never saw my son do (until recently) was *make or receive a phone call!* It would hardly be fair to compare the two "phones."

See the disconnect? When some advisors think of the reverse mortgage, they envision the equivalent of my 1997 cell phone. It was useful and timely for the era but limited in scope when compared with modern resources. However, today's newly re-structured Home Equity Conversion Mortgage (HECM) is much more like my son's smartphone. It has a myriad of applications, or "apps," that can help advisors create new and powerful retire-ment outcomes.

What Do You See: Investment, Asset, or Something Else Entirely?

What do you see when you look at the image to the left? Some perceive a house or a home, others say they see their client's biggest investment. I don't see a client investment; I see the clients' largest non-performing asset!

Equity is like finding an oil reserve in your backyard; it's only as valuable as its ability to be used.

Home equity means nothing to retirement unless it can be un-locked, and when it is unlocked, something happens. It turns into something entirely different: housing wealth!

Let's look at the five ways housing assets can be used to enhance retirement.

 Increasing Cash Flow: Would any of your clients say they have NO interest in learning how to have more accessible cash for their monthly enjoyment and expenses in retirement?

 Reducing Risks: Is there a safety net, backup plan, or insurance policy for everything that can go sideways in re-tirement? If there were, then certainly all your clients would want you to tell them about it.

 Preserving Assets: There are all types of eroding factors that can eat away at retirement savings. Some are out of our clients' control, but not all. Possessing this indispensable resource would be a game-changer for your clients, and not telling your clients about it would be indefensible!

 Improving Liquidity: "Time is filled with swift transition," said the old song we crooned growing up. The what-ifs will happen. What client would NOT want to learn of a way to have readily accessible access to tax-free dollars when unexpected events occur?

 Adding New Dollars to Savings: Do I even need to discuss this one? With the current savings rate and longevity crisis, I think it's reasonable to say that all your clients would want to know how they could accomplish this.

Now What Do You See?

Now what do you see when you look at the picture? You've observed the first way in which housing wealth has changed the retirement income conversation. It has changed the way you *see* the housing asset. The home is no longer an investment, but a powerful, five-fold retirement-enhancing resource that can transform your clients' retirement outcomes.

Once you see it, you will never view the retiree's house the same way again (or at least I hope not).

HOUSING WEALTH: The unlocked and guaranteed access to the appreciating equity in a retiree's home without the requirement of a monthly mortgage payment on the used portion.

The 5 Functions of Housing Wealth

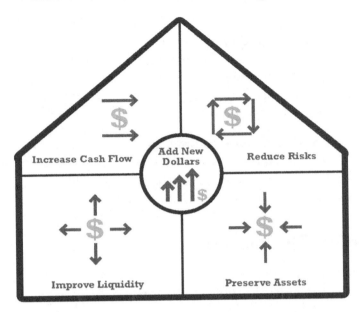

The Many Faces of Housing Wealth

- Housing wealth is a **revolutionary new term** that allows you as the advisor to engage in an entirely new stream of retirement planning conversations without using the term "reverse mortgages" to introduce the concepts. It opens planning doors with existing clients and expands your potential with new or emerging clients.

- Housing wealth is a **conversation bridge** that allows you to speak to younger clients about their aging loved ones and the ability they may have to create a more enjoyable retirement because of the presence of a home.

- Housing wealth can be **an additional asset class** like stocks, bonds, real estate holdings, global equities, cash positions, etc. Just as a client would not have all their money in stocks or CDs, so it would be with housing wealth. As an asset class, housing wealth can be incorporated into client review meetings when discussing risk management, portfolio rebalancing, and asset allocation for a more sustainable retirement.

- Housing wealth can become an **insurance policy** to transfer the risk of loss. It is a powerful hedging tool against the most common and devastating retirement risks: longevity, inflation, volatility, sequence, market risk, etc.

- Housing wealth can be used to **manage income and tax brackets**. Keeping clients within lower adjusted gross income boundaries reduces Medicare expenses, Social Security taxation, and overall income tax.

- Housing wealth as **inflation protection**: One of the most devastating things that can happen in retirement is inflation eroding savings and purchasing power. Having a certain amount of savings in vehicles that can keep pace with and exceed inflation is essential but carries some risk as well. You will see how housing wealth can serve as a powerful hedge against this risk.

- Housing wealth **converts a potential liability into an asset**. The home is a liability if the monthly debt servicing is creating unnecessary financial strain in retirement. It's an asset if it can be unlocked and used to create cash flow, reduce risks, preserve assets, enhance liquidity, or add new dollars into savings.

- Housing wealth is a **differentiator**. It sets the knowledgable advisor apart from the myriad of advisors who have no idea how to use it, or who dismiss housing wealth entirely.

What if Steve Jobs Had Seen a Different Demonstration

Imagine that it wasn't Steve Jobs, but it was you. Rather than a computer mouse, picture yourself looking at a demonstration of the ways the home could be used in retirement.

In the presentation, you would see the legacy planning strategy which advocated retirees sacrifice as much as possible in order to leave the home "mortgage free" to their heirs. You would be shown the traditional home loan strategy that encouraged retirees to borrow from the home to meet certain retirement needs but also required making monthly payments. Next you would observe a downsizing strategy that allowed retirees to generate new retirement dollars by selling their existing home and using the remaining proceeds (if sufficient) to buy a smaller home or rent an apartment.

But lastly, the presenter would show you the Housing Wealth strategy that allowed retirees to use their homes to increase cash flow, reduce retirement risks, preserve assets, improve liquidity and even add new dollars back into their savings all without ever having to make a monthly loan payment!

Imagine!

In February of 2018, the reverse mortgage turned thirty years old. Its ability to transform the retirement outcomes of tens of millions of existing retirees and emerging baby boomers is without measure. Yet it requires vision to see its untapped potential. Perhaps the same type of vision Steve Jobs had when he looked at the wooden box with a red button and saw that this could change the world.

Here's to having vision and not just sight.

> "If Xerox had known what it had and had taken advantage of its real opportunities it could have been as big as I.B.M. plus Microsoft plus Xerox combined—and the largest high-technology company in the world."
>
> *- Steve Jobs*

2

Eight Reasons Reverse Mortgages Are Gaining Advisors' Attention

I might talk about reverse mortgages if my clients brought it up, but they never have. Why should I mention it if they are not interested?

I've heard about reverse mortgages in reference to the DOL ruling and the Best-Interest Standard of Care ... what do they have to do with those practices?

I'm curious; would talking about reverse mortgages help or hurt my chances of "winning" a new client?

I've been reading more positive articles about reverse mortgages, but I still have some reservations. Is the excitement around the topic a passing trend?

My clients already have sufficient savings. How would a reverse mortgage help them?

A 2017 *New York Post* article reported, "On average, Americans check their phone once every twelve minutes, or about eighty times a day, with one in ten checking their phones on average once every four minutes." We all have things constantly vying for our attention, and advisors are no different. With the competition for your time, why should an advisor pay attention to reverse mortgages? In this chapter, we'll discuss eight reasons this investigation is worth your time and energy.

1. The Intersection of Housing Wealth and Retirement Planning

In the last chapter, we introduced the many faces of housing wealth. In the remainder of the book, we will explore how the intersection of housing wealth and retirement planning creates unprecedented opportunities to enhance retirement outcomes and efficiencies. By far, this is the number-one reason advisors are paying attention.

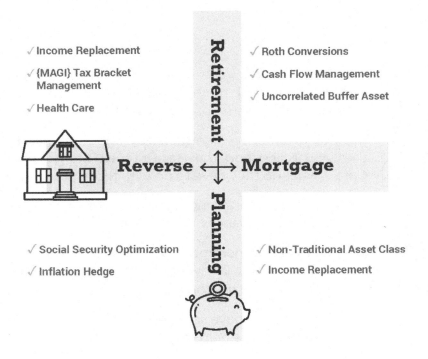

Mini Case Study: "The Rule of 30" vs. "The 4% Rule"

When most advisors or clients think about their net worth, they tend to consider their income, investments, insurance, and annuities, but they don't think of their housing wealth. This severely limits the scope of retirement planning conversations you can have with your clients, but if you begin incorporating housing wealth into the dialogue, a new world can emerge. Let's look at an example.

In 2017, Dr. Barry Sacks, Ph.D., introduced a paper in the *Journal of Financial Planning* called "Integrating Home Equity and Retirement Savings through the 'Rule of 30.'"

The article shows a way of determining how much retirement income a retiree can draw each year throughout a thirty-year retirement, specifically in situations where the retiree's principal sources of retirement income are a portfolio of securities and a home that does not have a traditional mortgage.

The research concludes that establishing a reverse mortgage at the onset of retirement and using the "Coordinated Draw Strategy" (discussed in chapter 8) extends the savings. The "Rule of 30" suggests that if you add the value of the portfolio (at the outset of retirement) to the value of the home (also at the outset of retirement) and then divide the sum by thirty, you will find the amount of the initial withdrawal that can be taken in the first year of retirement. In the subsequent years, the withdrawal will be the same amount, but adjusted for the previous year's inflation.

The Potential of Incorporating Housing Wealth

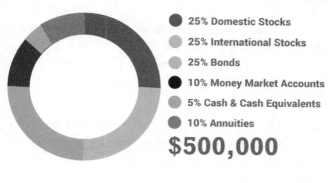

- 25% Domestic Stocks
- 25% International Stocks
- 25% Bonds
- 10% Money Market Accounts
- 5% Cash & Cash Equivalents
- 10% Annuities

$500,000

Initial Safe Withdrawal Rate
$20,000/yr.

$400,000

Initial Withdrawal Rate
$30,000/yr.

CASE EXAMPLE: Incorporating Housing Wealth to Add $10,000/Year to Client's Income

Advisor A: Using a standard 4 percent initial safe withdrawal rate on the $500,000 portfolio will provide an initial yearly income of $20,000 for their client.

Advisor B: Incorporating housing wealth ($400,000) and the existing portfolio ($500,000) creates a total wealth figure of $900,000. The advisor then applies the "Sacks Rule of 30," which uses the reverse mortgage coordination strategy and divides the total wealth of $900,000 by thirty to obtain a new sustainable initial withdrawal rate of $30,000/year for the client.

In this simple example, you can see how incorporating housing wealth can increase retirement outcomes and client satisfaction. Throughout the remainder of the book, we will continue to explore and unpack strategies that allow you to impact more clients, acquire new ones, and differentiate yourself from the ordinary advisor.

2. The Wide-Ranging Acceptance of the Program

The impact of reverse mortgages as part of the retirement income conversation is no longer an addendum. Many reputable institutions, individuals and organizations have come to embrace the program as a viable retirement income tool to be incorporated into planning.

"The use of a HECM {reverse mortgage} can reduce the cash reserve that we recommend a retiree hold from two years to six months ... providing a ready pool of capital to tap into when needed at a relatively low cost ... Our studies indicate this will significantly increase the survivability of the portfolio in retirement." **– Harold Evensky, Ph.D., Editorial Review Board, Journal of Financial Planning**

"Reverse mortgages are a powerful yet largely untapped tool for retirees to improve their standard of living. This is going to become one of the key means of funding retirement in the future." **– Dr. Robert C. Merton, Nobel Laureate and Professor of Finance, M.I.T.**

"If you had dismissed reverse mortgages in the past ... they're worth a second look. Otherwise, you may be missing out on a crucial way to improve clients' retirement security." **– Wade Pfau, Ph.D., Professor of Retirement, The American College of Financial Services**

Publications (partial list)

- The Journal of Financial Planning: "Standby Reverse Mort-gages: A Risk Management Tool for Retirement Distributions" and "Incorporating Home Equity into a Retirement Income Strategy"

- The Society of Financial Service Professionals: "Can Reverse Mortgages Hedge the Most Common Retirement Income Risks?" and "Housing Choices and Their Impact on Retirement Income Sustainability"

- Forbes: "Improving Retirement Income Efficiency Using Reverse Mortgages" and "Using Reverse Mortgages in A Re-sponsible Retirement Income Plan"

- Journal of Retirement: "The Reverse Mortgage: A Strategic Lifetime Income Planning Resource"

- The Stanford Center on Longevity: "Optimizing Retirement Income by Integrating Retirement Plans, IRAs, and Home Equity"

Most major financial advisor associations have featured reverse mortgage trainings, webinars, and workshops over the last year. The 2017 Financial Planning Association's conference had four different reverse mortgage-focused sessions. NAIFA, SFSP, NAPFA, and others have all included trainings recently. Schools such as The American College of Financial Services, Texas Tech, Ohio State, MIT Business School, and Boston College's Center for Retirement Research have all been favorably disposed towards the newly restructured reverse mortgage.

3. The Presence of Fierce Competition

There are only a handful of advisors who are unconcerned about client attrition, new client attraction, and standing out from the crowd. For the rest, these issues are paramount. The competition for your clients' attention is fierce, and the strategies to attract new clients are scarce. Adding housing wealth to your vocabulary, client-engagement strategies, and digital profile will certainly set you apart.

4. The Fiduciary Fallout of the Department of Labor Ruling

By the time you read this book, the specifics of the Department of Labor fiduciary standard ruling may or may not have teeth, but the fallout associated with it will. There is a growing awareness that advisors have a responsibility to do what is in the best interest of their clients. Part of that responsibility means staying informed about current thoughts, trends, and legitimate resources that could have a positive (or negative) effect upon clients meeting their retirement goals.

I believe that the newly restructured reverse mortgage qualifies as a legitimate resource that can optimize your clients' retirement outcomes and leaving this resource out of the retirement planning conversations could lead to less-than-optimal results. Dr. C.W. Copeland, professor of insurance and retirement income, said it best:

> *Advisors have a fiduciary responsibility to their clients. In no uncertain terms, this means that they must do what is in the best interest of their clients. If an advisor fails to become informed about the benefits of HECMs, they are failing at their fiduciary duty. By no means is an HECM right for every client, but every advisor worth their salt should have a cursory knowledge of the subject matter in order to, at a minimum, factor it out of their client's equation.*

5. The Profile of the New Borrowers

The reverse mortgage is no longer *only* for the house rich, cash poor. In the early years of my practice, AARP had a reverse mortgage video with the tag line, "If you consider yourself house rich but cash poor, a reverse mortgage could be the answer you're looking for." Though this was never indicative of the majority of borrowers, the idea stuck.

Since that time, numerous uses of the reverse mortgage have been developed—strategies that favor those who have healthy home equity *and* a healthy portfolio. Although the "house rich, cash poor" borrower can still benefit from a reverse mortgage, they are just one type of borrower.

Let's take a closer look at the five different types of retirement-age homeowners who are benefitting from the new reverse mortgage

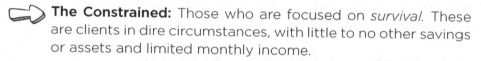 **The Constrained:** Those who are focused on *survival.* These are clients in dire circumstances, with little to no other savings or assets and limited monthly income.

The Concerned: Those who are focused on *rescuing* retirement income. The client's retirement plan has encountered something unexpected. Perhaps one spouse had planned to work longer but couldn't, or an unexpected health crisis drains the savings faster than expected.

I once had a client whose wife was a very successful real estate agent. Though she was sixty-two, her business was booming, and she had no intent on retiring until one day when she was suddenly unable to speak. A neurological phenomenon had taken her voice with no medical remedy available. She decided to wait it out and see what would happen, but in the interim, the couple's retirement plan needed a rescue.

The Cautious: Those who are focused on increasing *contingency.* In this case, a client has a workable retirement plan but not enough reserved for the unexpected or undesirable: prolonged poor markets, higher-than-expected inflation, unwise portfolio draws during bear markets, etc.

The Comfortable: Those who are focused on *improving* retirement plans. These clients have a workable (or nearly workable) retirement plan but desire enhancement: increased retirement spending, the creation of a hedge for market corrections, establishment of legacy gifting with asset protection, and life insurance.

The Carefree: These are the Bill Gates, the Warren Buffets of the world. They are not going to run out of money—ever.

Why would a retired CEO who had $5 million in investments and was living in a $4 million home be inquiring about a reverse mortgage? This client of mine had nearly $2 million in housing debt with a monthly mortgage payment more than $20,000.

The newly restructured reverse mortgage is designed to create new planning conversations from the clients you may consider carefree to the ones you know are not.

6. The Clients Who Are Already Asking

It's been estimated that a quarter million people bought a drill last year. The irony is most of those buyers didn't actually want a drill; *they wanted a hole!* The drill was just the tool needed to achieve the goal.

In the same way, there are challenges in your clients' retirement that they know need to be overcome; they just don't know the names of all the tools available to solve them. Many advisors have now realized that their clients have been asking about reverse mortgages for years; they just didn't use the term "reverse mortgage."

For example, have your clients ever asked about refinancing or eliminating their loan payment, so they can reduce their current draw or have extra money to enjoy retirement? Have they ever wanted to annuitize prematurely or cannibalize an asset because of a spending shock? Have clients shown concern about their savings being vulnerable to a market correction, or to erosion that comes with inflation?

They are describing the problem and looking to you to produce the right tool to solve it. In many cases, today's reverse mortgage can be a handy tool, but many of your clients are unfamiliar with what it does, so they don't know to even ask for it.

7. The Baby Boomers' Major Retirement Problems

This generation will live longer, save less, and carry more debt into retirement than past generations. You are responsible for crafting a plan that will get them through the finish line. I will spend more time on this later, but suffice it to say, this group is not well prepared for a lengthy retirement. Still, they do have something unique that no other generation has had before them: housing wealth.

8. The Size of the Home Equity Opportunity

It's been noted that nearly 100 percent of existing retirees and emerging baby boomers have already seen, heard of, or inquired about reverse mortgages—with more than 90 percent having a favorable response toward them. Recent findings also demonstrate that only 16 percent of baby boomers have a written retirement plan or someone they consider a personal advisor.

In addition to this, there are currently more than $6 trillion dollars in senior home equity! If you are not incorporating housing wealth into your planning conversations, you are missing out on the single largest way for you to impact current clients, access new ones and grow your practice.

With so much vying for your attention, I am glad you have taken the time to read this book. I think you'll find it is worth the investment of your energy, especially considering the planning challenges ahead as more and more baby boomers retire every day. In the next chapter, we will explore just what those challenges are and why the boomers have made your job harder.

3

Mick Jagger, Michelle Obama, and Donald Trump:

The Face of Today's Retirement

I keep hearing baby boomer and reverse mortgage in the same sentence. What is it about that generation that keeps bringing up the topic?

How does adding housing wealth to the traditional retirement sources of wealth change outcomes?

What is the difference between retirement planning and retirement income planning? Is the difference significant or semantics?

I know a substantial part of my clients' total wealth is tied up in their homes; how much does that impact their retirement savings plan?

Mick Jagger, Michelle Obama, and Donald Trump.

What do these three have in common? They each represent today's retiree. Jagger, born in 1943, is the face of existing retirees, while the other two (born between 1946 and 1964) represent the baby boomers.

Three Boomer Themes That Have Changed Retirement Planning as We Know It

If there's one generation in recent history that has most dramatically changed the retirement planning game, it's the baby boomers. They're one of the most talked-about generations today, with a host of well-documented challenges facing them. Three overarching themes stand out in particular:

- **They will live longer than previous generations.** Instead of spanning fifteen or twenty years, their retirement will last twenty-five, thirty, or even thirty-five years or more. A longer retirement necessitates additional funding; add inflation and global economic uncertainty to the mix, and you've got one expensive quarter-century to plan for.

- **They will carry more consumer debt into retirement than previous generations.** Much of the boomers' money in retirement will be tied up in debt they accumulated during their working years. Someone once said a boomer never met a credit card they didn't like. This can be especially problematic when retirees move to a fixed income.

- **They have not saved enough money to sustain their retirement needs.** The most talked-about fact of all is that the majority of baby boomers have not saved enough to sustain retirement income for their projected lifespan. Even an attempt to increase saving in the years leading up to retirement will not make up for the compounding interest that could have been earned over the course of their careers.

The boomer generation is struggling to prepare for retirement and will continue to do so over the next fifteen years (until all in the generation reach retirement age). The statistics are alarming; here are ten facts recently released by the Insured Retirement Institute (IRI):

√ Only 24 percent of baby boomers are confident they will have enough savings to last throughout retirement (down from 36 percent in 2012).

√ Of the baby boomers who lack confidence, 68 percent said they would have saved more, and 67 percent said they would have started earlier when asked what they would have done differently.

√ Just 39 percent of baby boomers have tried to figure out their retirement savings need.

√ Only 55 percent of baby boomers have any money saved for retirement. In fairness, however, one in four baby boomers expects significant income from an employer-provided pension.

√ Fifty-nine percent of baby boomers cite Social Security as a major source of their retirement income.

√ Sixty-five percent of baby boomers are worried about future changes to Social Security.

√ Only 43 percent of baby boomers are satisfied with how their lives are going from an economic perspective.

√ Twenty-six percent of baby boomers don't plan to retire until age seventy or later.

√ Only 22 percent of baby boomers believe they are doing a good job of preparing financially for retirement.

√ Only 27 percent of baby boomers believe they will have enough money for health care expenses.

Yikes. This is a horrifying list but truthful nonetheless. What does it indicate? *Baby boomers are in danger of running out of money during retirement.* Unless advisors find new ways and new tools to help them cope, the financial impact will be devastating.

Recently, I heard retirement specialist and heavyweight Tom Hegna share a story with some very powerful truths relevant to the predicament of boomers. The original story is from Dick Austin and can be found in Hegna's book, *Retirement Income Masters: Secrets of the Pros*. A portion is reprinted below.

The Parable of the Last Mile

 Some friends from the Northeast had always wanted to visit the desert, so they flew to Death Valley, rented a car and headed across the desert. The trip was wonderful! Everyone was having a great time, but suddenly, they noticed a road sign that read, "Next Gas Station 100 Miles" . . . and their gas gauge was rapidly approaching "E." Their joy quickly turned to anguish, and they worried about what they should do.

Just as the friends stared at the glaring red "E," many people in retirement are staring at their own "gas gauge"—their brokerage or savings account balance—waiting for it to run out. Unfortunately, life for many brings about the loss of peace of mind in retirement and the inability to enjoy the "scenery" along the way.

Running out of money in retirement is just like running out of fuel. Everyone thinks it's about the day you run out. But it's really about the years prior to that unfortunate event. It can be said, "You know you're going to run out, but you just don't know when. – Dick Austin

. . . stay tuned for the surprising conclusion of the journey.

Climbing Retirement Mountain

Retirement planning has always been viewed as a journey. Most recently, it has been compared to climbing Mount Everest—a metaphor that leaves no illusions regarding the challenges faced. It requires preparation, precision, and training, and while it may be an arduous journey, the experience of other climbers has taught us that a successful (and enjoyable) climb is attainable.

Traditionally, retirement planning was focused on getting the client to the top of the mountain. This was commonly referred to as the **Accumulation Phase**, and its primary focus was on asset allocation. This was generally accomplished by diversifying holdings among different types of investments to balance risks and rewards. The goal was for the clients to work while able, save all they could, protect as much as possible to get to the top of the mountain, retire, and then live off what they had amassed.

The second part of the journey was the descent, known as the **Distribution Phase.** It necessitates a strategy for income allocation—diversifying income among a variety of sources—each designed to provide unique benefits for different income objectives.

However, the advent of the baby boomers has given rise to a much different reality. The retirement mountain was much higher than they expected. Working longer, spending less, and saving more are now the rules versus the exceptions. For many, seventy is the new sixty-two.

The other reality is that coming down the mountain is more dangerous than going up! Nearly two-thirds of the mountain-climbing deaths that occurred on Mt. Everest happened on the way down! The danger doesn't dissipate upon reaching the summit and planting the flag; *it increases.* This also proves true with retirement. It's not getting to the top but getting back to base camp that is the most dangerous.

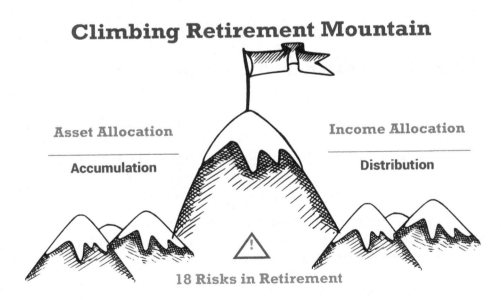

Climbing Retirement Mountain

Asset Allocation

Accumulation

Income Allocation

Distribution

18 Risks in Retirement

Eighteen Risks that Can Derail Retirement

The American College has identified eighteen major risks distinctly associated with and amplified by descending the retirement mountain. Some scholars suggest twelve and others twenty-six, but no matter the precise number, the danger is nonetheless very real. (www.18risks.com)

1. Longevity Risk
2. Inflation Risk
3. Excessive Withdrawal Risk
4. Health Expense Risk
5. Long-Term Care Risk
6. Market Risk
7. Fragility Risk
8. Financial Elder Abuse Risk
9. Interest Rate Risk
10. Liquidity Risk
11. Sequence of Returns Risk
12. Forced Retirement Risk
13. Re-Employment Risk
14. Employer Insolvency Risk
15. Loss of Spouse Risk
16. Unexpected Financial Responsibility Risk
17. Timing Risk
18. Public Policy Risk

Question: How do we approach retirement planning considering these new and dangerous realities?

In 2012, the American College of Financial Services endeavored to answer this question. At a summit of financial thought leaders, and through a series of interviews, they sought to find consensus on the best practices for coming down the retirement mountain, especially in light of the boomers' increased longevity, lower savings, and higher debt.

After the research was completed, a new term was coined to capture and synthesize the best practices. The name of the new discipline was **Retirement Income Planning,** with the focus being on "income," and the new designation was called the Retirement Income Certified Professional (RICP®). No longer solely focused on climbing the mountain, the emphasis was now on using all available tools and strategies for getting the clients safely back to base camp.

The Advisor's Traditional Tools

For years, advisors have had three primary sources of client wealth to work with:

- The **Income** Bucket (Social Security, pension, employment)
- The **Investment** Bucket (IRA, 401k, 403b, etc.)
- The **Insurance** Bucket (annuities, life insurance, business to be sold in future, second home, etc.)

It was from these available sources that advisors transformed client wealth into lifetime income, while attempting to lessen risk and meet the retirement expectations of their clients.

Question: Are these three pockets of wealth and traditional tools enough to mitigate the risks with the current descent retirees are facing?

To answer, let's go back to our friends in the desert to see if they reached their destination.

What Happened to the Friends in the Desert?

As the friends reached the peak of dismay, someone recalled that this particular model had a reserve tank. The switch should be easily accessible in the glove compartment.

"No way," one proclaimed.

Another said, "I heard about that, but thought that was only on the more expensive models."

"It can't be. If that were true, the rental agent would surely have mentioned it!"

"Let's open up the glove compartment and see."

To their amazement, there it was. Once they activated it, the gas gauge showed that the car could safely reach the next gas station.

What a relief! The passengers took a deep breath, and their trip was once again enjoyable.

As the travelers continued to read about this reserve tank, they discovered that their last-minute activation of the reserve tank was the least efficient way to use it. The reserve system had been designed to enhance the efficiency of gas usage and employing it as a last resort was actually less efficient.

They also discovered:

- The main gas tank alone could take the vehicle about 500 miles.

- Turning on the reserve gas tank **AFTER** the main tank was nearly empty added about **75 miles**.

- If they had used the reserve tank **FIRST** and **THEN** switched to the main tank, the vehicle would have gone an extra **180 miles**.

- If they had switched back and forth between the two tanks based on the varying conditions outside, they could have gotten an extra **300 miles**.

What a crazy story. Unbelievable, right? Counterintuitive and almost illogical, but the point is clearly visible. Retirement is a long journey. There is a reserve gas tank outfitted for 87 percent of "vehicles."

The reverse mortgage is the equivalent of the reserve gas tank in the parable!

- It's designed for a long journey.

- It's accessible to about 87 percent of retirees.

- When properly used, it can make a huge difference in the outcomes of consumers.

As mentioned earlier, recent surveys say that 87 percent of boomers and existing retirees own their home. In addition, the U.S. Census Bureau states that the average retiring sixty-five-year-old couple will have *68 percent of their total wealth* tied up in their home equity. For most, that nearly doubles their amount of assets.

Equity and Non-Equity Assets

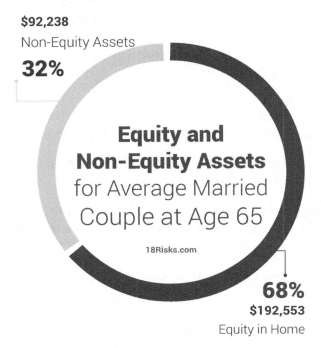

$92,238
Non-Equity Assets

32%

**Equity and
Non-Equity Assets**
for Average Married
Couple at Age 65

18Risks.com

68%
$192,553
Equity in Home

Simply stated, the average boomer is living in their biggest asset and most significant source of their total wealth. In the context of the current savings and longevity crisis, plus more than $6 trillion in accessible senior home equity, doesn't integrating housing wealth into a retirement income plan just make sense?

> *"Retirees simply cannot afford to continue to ignore home equity as an income source and still meet their retirement goals." – **Professor Jamie Hopkins***

So how do reverse mortgages and retirement savings *work together* to enhance retirement outcomes and client satisfaction?

Fortunately, with the rise and development of retirement *income* planning, housing wealth can now play the role it was created to play: serving as an additional tool to help increase the security and longevity of retirement savings during the descent. It can be added to the three income buckets to bolster income allocation by increasing efficiencies.

The 4 Pockets

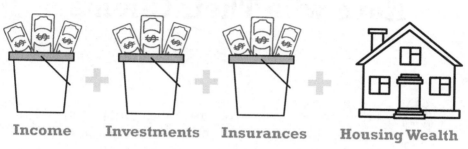

| Income | Investments | Insurances | Housing Wealth |

Like the parable, many advisors don't know or won't talk about the reserve gas tank, and those who do know about its existence usually don't know how to use it effectively. They mistakenly propose that their clients wait until they run out of assets before establishing a reverse mortgage. Recent research advises this is absolutely the worst way to use the program.

The travelers in the SUV were beside themselves that the rental agent (who knew of their long journey) had not told them about every safety option. Your clients, too, will show the same disappointment if you are not giving them every resource available for their long retirement journey.

Advisors cannot afford to be wrong about housing wealth! There is too much at stake, and it's too easy to get it right.

4

The Five Most Important Conversations Advisors Should Have with Their Clients

I don't know how to initiate conversations regarding reverse mortgages with my clients in a natural way. How would you suggest going about it?

I already have an intake/annual review question-naire. Why would you advocate incorporating your questions?

How do we incorporate housing wealth into the retirement income conversation?

The title of this book says there are three ways in which reverse mortgages have changed the retirement conversation. If you recall, the first way is how they've changed the way we **SEE** the housing asset—no longer as an investment or non-producing asset, but as a means to increase cash flow, reduce risks, preserve assets, improve liquidity, and add new investable dollars back into savings.

In this chapter, we will cover the second major shift that reverse mortgages have provided in the retirement income conversation: reverse mortgages have changed the way advisors **SOLVE** the five most pressing retirement concerns.

We know that retirement will last longer, and existing retirees/emerging boomers have some troublesome challenges ahead. Where to begin? How do we broach the conversation?

An advisor recently sent me this email:

> *Don, we first met at a seminar two years ago. You discussed the HECM Line of Credit option for a safety net as a viable financial tool for clients. To be honest, I have spent the last two years working on my already busy practice. I have asked a few older advisors and their thoughts were reverse mortgages are the devil. I also reached out to multiple banks and all of them said the same, "We don't do those because they are bad for clients." I even broached the conversation with a few really good clients in their early 60s. They agreed they should get more info based on my explanation (which was to say, I know if used properly they aren't the devil). With all that said, my real question is, what's the next step? How do I explain and get clients to see the benefits of a HECM?*

What a great email! I was struck by the honesty and persistence of this advisor. Even amid discouragement from older advisors and banks, he knew that the reverse mortgage was valuable. What he didn't know was how to incorporate its principles into retirement income conversations. It reminds me of a young fellow who builds up the courage to get a young lady's number but doesn't know quite what to do next.

In my twenty years of working with clients, I've found the best place to start is with client expectations. What are the best ways to explore and unveil them? Questions. Thought-provoking, laser-focused questions reveal your clients' expectations, concerns, and openness to change.

I suspect that most who are reading this book already use an initial consultation/periodic review questionnaire to accomplish those goals. Recently, though, I've been encouraging advisors to use a framework that is simple to understand and extremely powerful when combined with laser-focused questions. It can be easily added to what you may already be doing.

These concepts are also foundational for the rest of the book. They are the lens by which we view retirement and the bedrock on which we build every case study. You will see the corresponding symbols throughout the chapters as it represents the starting and ending point of incorporating the housing wealth conversation into your practice.

The conversations are centered around the five core concerns retirees have (often referred to as the 5 Ls): **Longevity, Lifestyle, Liquidity, Legacy,** and **Long-Term Care.** The subsequent inquiries are designed to generate additional dialogue. Although I will include just one question for each concern, I'd encourage you to develop as many thought-provoking questions around the subject matter as you can. The more questions, the better.

The 5 L's

Let's examine each of the five core conversations.

The Longevity Conversation: "Will I have enough savings to meet my basic living expenses?"

According to most surveys, the number-one concern of retirees continues to be "running out of savings." The advisor's primary focus must be on the lifetime survival of clients' savings to meet essential living requirements: food, housing, medical expenses, etc.

Clearly, there are many things that can erode a nest egg, including market fluctuation, sequence risks, inflation, excessive withdrawals, and unexpected expenses. The bottom line remains: running out of money and not being a burden on family is still at the forefront of every retiree's mind.

To determine if longevity is a priority for your clients, ask the following question: **On a scale of 1 to 10, how much does the thought of running out of savings in retirement trouble you?**

The Lifestyle Conversation: "Will I have enough money to enjoy retirement on my terms?"

It's one thing to have enough savings to meet your basic needs, but it's another to maintain your desired overall standard of living and not be forced to make moderate to drastic lifestyle changes. These lifestyle components tend to be more discretionary in nature and may include things like travel and leisure, self-improvement activities, social engagements, and helping a family member.

My friend Dr. Wade Pfau suggests that maximizing spending power is the key to meeting this concern. Spending can remain consistent and sustainable while allowing for an acceptable degree of risk. Furthermore, clients must keep in mind that these expenses may need to be scaled back at certain points in retirement.

Regardless of the components, lifestyle goals can be revealing when it comes to your clients' retirement expectations. To determine if lifestyle is a priority for your clients, try asking them the following question: **On a scale of 1 to 10, how disappointed would you be if you had to adjust your standard of living to make your savings last?**

The Legacy Conversation: "How will I be financially remembered?"

How will you be financially remembered? This is my definition of legacy. Traditionally, legacy goals relate to leaving assets for subsequent generations, or to charities. However, I believe it includes significantly more.

Perhaps your clients won't have to borrow money from their children, move into their son's spare bedroom, or ask their daughter to quit working to care for them. To determine if legacy is a priority for your clients, try asking them the following question: **On a scale of 1 to 10, how important is it for you to cut back on your** retirement lifestyle if it meant leaving more legacy for your heirs and not having to rely on them, financially or otherwise?

The Liquidity Conversation: "Will I have access to tax-advantaged money when I need it?"

Maintaining additional assets that can be tapped quickly to provide funds for unexpected contingencies is critical in retirement. Ideally, these reserves should be accessible with as little taxable or opportunity-loss impact as possible.

The liquidity conversation is focused on such run-of-the-mill spending shocks as emergencies, expenses, unexpected illnesses, or death. Essentially, this involves something that you want or need to buy but don't want to liquidate savings to do it. The "what ifs" of retirement are endless and having access to a reserve for the inevitable is essential.

To determine if liquidity is a priority for your clients, ask them: **On a scale of 1 to 10, how prepared are you for unexpected spending shocks in retirement?**

The Long-Term Care Conversation: "Am I financially prepared for the costs of health-related expenses?"

A 2017 study by Fidelity Investments said that a couple retiring that year would need an estimated $275,000 to cover out-of-pocket health care costs in retirement. That's a 6 percent increase over the prior year's estimates and significantly more than 2014. Some experts have even suggested that this figure was low!

This estimate applies to those with traditional Medicare insurance coverage and considers premiums, co-payments, deductibles, and out-of-pocket drug costs. It does not consider the cost of a nursing home or long-term care that clients may need; long-term care alone is estimated to be an additional $130,000. I have found this expense to be the one that most folks ignore almost completely.

Originally, I was not planning to give this concern its own conversation, but because of the enormity of the expense and how often it is overlooked and dismissed, I chose to make it a separate category.

To determine if long-term care is a priority for your clients, try asking them the following question: **On a scale of 1 to 10, how prepared would you be if you had to access an additional $300,000 for health care-related costs?**

Five Client Questions:

How much does the thought of running out of savings in retirement trouble you?

How disappointed would you be if you had to adjust your standard of living in order to make your savings last?

How willing would you be to give up or cut back on your retirement lifestyle, if it meant leaving more legacy for your heirs?

How prepared are you for unexpected spending shocks in retirement?

How prepared would you be if you had to access an additional $300,000 for health care related costs?

All five of these concerns are a daily part of the boomers' and existing retirees' retirement reality. Throughout the remainder of this book, especially in the case studies, I will refer to the 5Ls and their accompanying conversations/questions. Everything will be filtered through these, and as we move forward, you will indeed see how reverse mortgages have changed the way advisors **SOLVE** the five most pressing retirement concerns!

SECTION 2:

THE NEW REVERSE MORTGAGE

Understanding the Newly Restructured
Reverse Mortgage: What's New, What's Not,
Alternatives, and Misconceptions

5

Four Words that Instantly Ease Reverse Mortgage Concerns

(Understanding the Basics)

Sometimes I'm embarrassed to bring up reverse mortgages because of their reputation; is there a different way to understand them?

Is it true that clients can lose their home if they get a reverse mortgage?

What are the basics: who's eligible, how do you determine how much they receive, when is it paid back, do the heirs get anything, etc.?

If the sale of the house doesn't cover the reverse mortgage, are the kids responsible for paying the rest?

Have you ever been in room of people when someone mentions a reverse mortgage? Perhaps it was at a business meeting, a barber shop or a family gathering? If you have, you know that even an innocent comment can turn the best gathering into a chaotic disaster. The verbal sparring matches, the fearful silence, and the hearsay of horror stories are enough to make you think twice about sharing your thoughts.

Over the years, I have discovered that sharing four words about reverse mortgages can help put advisors and their clients at ease. What are these four words?

IT'S JUST A MORTGAGE!

It's true. Beneath the fear, suspicion, and myths lies one very simple truth about the reverse mortgage: **it's just a mortgage.**

A few years ago, I visited Detroit, Michigan, home of Ford Motors. While there, I discovered a massive art piece that chronicled all the basic Ford vehicles, from the 1908 Model T to the 2016 Focus. I found it very interesting that every car, regardless of year or model, shared a few basic features: four wheels, a braking mechanism, a steering wheel, and some sort of engine to power them. Apart from those things, they were very different, but the four features remained consistent throughout the years.

The same is true with reverse mortgages. They are part of the larger "mortgage" family, and when you peek "underneath the hood," you will discover four very important words: **it's just a mortgage!**

Look at it this way: most advisors are not concerned when a client wishes to obtain a home equity loan or line of credit to make home repairs, help the grandchildren, or go on a trip. These clients don't want to take money out of investments or savings, so they ask their advisor for a recommendation. The scenario is fairly common and very straightforward; nothing spooky so far.

To illustrate this point, let's outline the journey of two clients who each obtained a home equity loan. One secured a traditionally amortizing loan and the other a HECM reverse mortgage. Look closely.

 A Tale of Two Couples

✓ Both Asked Their Advisor About Home Equity Lines of Credit

✓ Both Went to a Lender

✓ Both Produced Income and Credit Qualifications

✓ Both Were Approved for a $100,000 Line of Credit

✓ Both were Told to Maintain Home, Pay Taxes and Keep Insurance in Force

✓ Both Used the Money

✓ Both Began Making Payments of the Exact Amount, Same Day, Same Interest Rate

✓ Both Paid Until Their Loan Balance Was Paid Off

Can you tell the difference? No, you can't because on the surface, both the traditional loan and the reverse mortgage function in exactly the same way. Why? Underneath it all, the reverse mortgage is just a mortgage!

Those four simple words have helped many advisors and their clients pause long enough to catch their breath, silence their fears, and take a closer look at the program. Once you remove reverse mortgages from "spooky land," you can be open to see how they work, how they are different, and how they are designed to be used.

The History of Housing Wealth

Equity release programs for seniors have been in existence for more than 100 years. After starting in England, they spread to numerous countries including Scotland, Ireland, China, Singapore, Australia, Indonesia, and Canada. Regardless of the location in the world you find them, the basic premise has always been the same: help an aging population sustain a longer retirement.

Across the globe, the home served as the largest financial asset for most retirees, but the means of accessing its value to enhance retirement outcomes was limited. One option was to sell the home, take out the cash, and move. The other option was the traditional home equity loan with its monthly payments. Both choices have value, but they didn't always meet the needs of most retirees. The overwhelming consensus was that most retirees want to stay in their own homes and don't want payments in their later years.

Enter the equity release program—a way to convert the home asset into retirement income. No moving or mandatory monthly payments involved. In the United States, these programs are called reverse mortgages, and there are three types that exist today:

- **Private Reverse Mortgages**. These began in the United States in 1961.

- **Jumbo Reverse Mortgages**. These are private equity release programs for higher-value or second homes. Typically, homes that benefit most from these are worth $1.2 million or more.

- **The Home Equity Conversion Mortgage** (**HECM**). In existence since 1988, these reverse mortgages are overseen by the United States Department of Housing and are insured by the Federal Housing Administration (FHA). Today, nearly 95 percent of all reverse mortgages are HECMs.

HECM Basics

For the sake of our discussion, we're going to be focusing on the Home Equity Conversion Mortgage (HECM). It is a federally insured, non-recourse loan (see repayment illustration) that allows people age sixty-two or older to convert a portion of their primary residence's value into tax-free dollars.

What are the basic eligibility qualifications?

To qualify, at least one borrowing spouse must be age sixty-two or older; the other need only be eighteen or older.

What type of properties qualify?

The loan can only be done on what is considered the primary residence. The property can be a single-family home, a HUD-approved condo, a manufactured home, or a one- to four-unit home with the condition that the client lives in one of the four units.

Are there financial/credit qualifications?

Borrowers will need to prove their willingness and capacity to meet their monthly obligations: property-related taxes, insurance, and any monthly mortgage payments. These must have been paid in a timely manner over the past twenty-four to thirty-six months. Furthermore, clients must retain a certain amount of residual monthly income after covering their basic housing obligations. If they don't, the lender can look at accumulated savings to satisfy that requirement, or they may reserve a portion of the HECM loan funds to pay the clients' taxes and insurances for a certain length of time.

How much can borrowers qualify for?

The amount of money a borrower is eligible for is based on three primary factors:

- **Age** of the youngest borrower

- **Value of the property,** up to the current lending limit ($679,650 at time of printing)

- **Interest rate** associated with the selected program

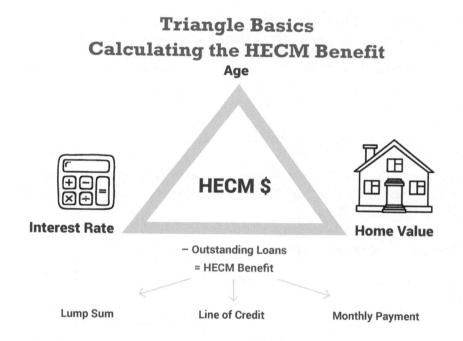

Triangle Basics
Calculating the HECM Benefit

Age

HECM $

Interest Rate

Home Value

− Outstanding Loans
= HECM Benefit

Lump Sum   Line of Credit   Monthly Payment

Does the home need to be free and clear?

A HECM must be a first mortgage. This means if you have a remaining mortgage or home equity loan balance, you are required to pay it prior to settlement, or use the HECM proceeds to pay it off before using the money in any other way.

How can proceeds be distributed?

There are five ways in which you can receive your money through a HECM:

- **Lump Sum:** As a protective feature, the borrower can only receive 60 percent of available benefit in the first year. The remainder can be received in subsequent years.

- **Line of Credit**: Like a home equity line of credit, you can tap into an increasing pool of money at any time when money is needed.

- **Regular Tenure Payments:** This is a regular monthly payment backed by the federal government and guaranteed to come to the borrower for as long as the loan is open.

- **Regular Term Payments:** A monthly payment of a set amount is received over a specific amount of time.

- **Hybrid**: This option is a combination of a lump sum (often used to pay off a mortgage) and monthly payments, with the line of credit functioning as a reserve.

You can get an approximate idea of how much you could receive through a HECM by using one of the many reverse mortgage online calculators. A very simple calculator that does not require email, phone number, or personal information can be found at www.HECMCalculator.net.

Does the borrower have any requirements?

There are four basic requirements the client must do to maintain the HECM reverse mortgage:

- The home must remain the **principal residence** of at least one of the borrowers. The client can own more than one residence, but only the primary residence can have a HECM placed against it.

- Client must **maintain the home** in a lendable condition. For example, they cannot allow a tree to fall through the roof and not get it repaired.

- Client must keep basic **homeowner's insurance** in force.

- Client must pay all **property-related taxes**.

The Number One Reason for Reverse Mortgage's Bad Rap

How did the reverse mortgage get such a bad reputation if those are the only requirements for maintaining the loan? Just watch the latest news broadcast: *Elderly Woman Gets Put Out of Home Over $0.27 in Reverse Mortgage.* Or read the latest newspaper heading: *Retired Couple Loses Home to Reverse Mortgage.* Frightening! What do you think is the number one reason the program ends up in the media with some horror story?

If you said clients not paying their property taxes, you would be correct.

The headlines are spooky, but what you'll find in nearly every case is the homeowners did not, would not or, in some cases, could not pay their property-related taxes. When this happens, it is the municipality who initiates action and informs the lender, who is then forced to act.

In other stories, there were salespeople who didn't see the program as a retirement income tool, but rather as a method for getting retirees what they wanted, even if it wasn't in their best interest. I've seen people use reverse mortgage proceeds to buy a new car or boat, to travel, to make home renovations, etc. While none of these are innately bad, they are problematic when isolated from the total picture, especially when they make money for emergencies or necessary expenses unavailable.

In some instances, unethical practitioners would have a younger spouse removed from the loan, so the family could get more money, without informing them of the consequences of doing such an action. Fortunately, the restructured program no longer allows this to happen.

Finally, in a few cases, there were reverse mortgage loan originators who were in cahoots with financial advisors. They encouraged clients to take the lump sum (or very large sum) of their HECM and purchase an equity fund, which could lose principal, or an annuity that often-carried steep surrender terms. Neither strategy is necessarily bad, but if it was not coordinated with other assets, it often left seniors without sufficient liquidity or caused tremendous stress because of the possibility of loss. Unfortunately, in some of those cases, one bad apple can spoil the bunch.

The restructured reverse mortgage (Reverse Mortgage Stabilization Act of 2013, 2015 HECM Financial Assessment and the 2017 HECM HUD overhaul) has solved many of the earlier problems by adding:

- **Greater Spousal Protection.** A younger spouse can remain on title and does not face displacement if the older spouse predeceases them.

- **Greater Equity Protections.** The new HUD overhaul benefits clients by reducing interest rates, allowing the loan to grow slowly and preserving more equity while still making sufficient initial dollars available.

- **Greater Scrutiny of Income and Credit.** The goal is to make sure the right retirees—those with a pattern of financial responsibility who understand the program's purpose—are given access to the program.

These safeguards have created tremendous improvement and confidence in the program. Unfortunately, there is no safeguard for irresponsible clients, the occasional misguided lender, or the rouge advisor, but the strengthening of the program and public accountability have gone a long way to make reverse mortgages a viable addition to retirement income plans.

Top Repayment Questions, Answers, and Examples

The HECM generally does not have to be repaid until the last surviving homeowner either passes away or permanently moves from the property. Even if a spouse passes away, the client has a right to remain in the home if they choose to do so.

Borrowers cannot be forced by a lender to sell their home (for the purpose of repayment) as long as the loan requirements are met, and they are allowed to remain in their home for as long as they like, even if the outstanding loan balance, plus interest, is more than the value of the property.

When does the loan get repaid?

When the home is no longer being used as a primary residence, the cash advances, interest, and other finance charges related to the reverse mortgage must be repaid to the lender. ALL remaining proceeds beyond the amount that are owed belong to the borrower, or the estate if the borrower is deceased. In the case of the borrower's death, the remaining equity can then be transferred to the heirs. NO debt is passed along to the beneficiaries.

In most cases, the home is sold, but if the family wishes to retain the home, they can use whatever means available to repay the lender, including life Insurance, other assets, or refinancing the HECM into a traditional loan. It doesn't matter to the lender, as long as the loan is paid.

HUD requires the repayment conversation to be initiated with the lender/servicer within thirty days of the last surviving borrower's permanent departure from the home. The executor will then have six months to settle the HECM. Extensions can be granted by HUD for an additional six months.

Repayment Example

- Client Age: 70 | Home Value: **$200,000** | Available Money Through HECM: $100,000 at an interest rate of 5 percent

- Outstanding Beginning Balance: **$100,000**

Take a look at the illustration:

HECM Reverse Mortgage Repayment

Years Home	Home Value	HECM Loan Balance	Remaining Equity
0	$200,000	$100,000	$100,000
10	$300,000	$163,000	$137,000
?		$400,000	

Day One: Clients' home is worth $200,000. They obtained a HECM and paid off their existing mortgage. After settlement, they now owe the HECM lender $100,000.

If they were to move or decease at the end of week one, the home would be sold and the $100,000 (plus one week's worth of interest) is owed. The remaining $100,000 will go to them if they move, or pass on to the heirs/estate if the client has deceased.

Ten Years Later: If the client stayed in the home for ten years and *chose not to make monthly payments*, the interest on the loan will have accrued, and their loan balance will be larger. On the chart, notice that in year ten, they owe the lender $163,000.

The chart also shows the $200,000 home appreciating at about 4 percent over those ten years. It's now worth $300,000. If they were to move or decease at this time, the home could be sold, the HECM paid off, and they (or their heirs) pocket the difference of $137,000.

How much will the clients owe in years fifteen, twenty, and twenty-five?

We may not know exactly what will happen in the future, but we can determine three possible scenarios:

- The client owes $400,000 at some point in the future, and the home is worth **$500,000**. They and/or the heirs will pocket $100,000 {$500k - $400k = $100k}.

- The client owes $400,000 at some point in the future, and the home is worth **$400,000**. They and/or the heirs will break even {$400k - $400k = $0}.

- The client owes $400,000 at some point in the future, and the home is worth **$300,000.** The client now owes more than the home is worth.

What does non-recourse loan mean?

Since the HECM reverse mortgage is an FHA Insured Non-Recourse Loan, the lender's ONLY "recourse" is the net proceeds from the sale of the home ($300,000), even though the client owes $400,000.

The FHA mortgage insurance fund bridges the difference. Neither the client nor their heirs/estate are responsible for repayment of the note, and no deficiency judgment can be taken either.

We've covered a lot in this chapter, and you should now know enough of the basic details of the reverse mortgage to be able to talk intelligibly about it. If nothing else, you know how to explain it in four words: **it's just a mortgage.**

6

The Eighth Wonder of the Financial World

What's the difference between a standard home equity line of credit and the reverse mortgage line of credit (ReLOC)? Which one would be better for my client?

I also read that HECMs have a guaranteed, tax-free growth rate; is that true? If so, how does it work? At what rate does it grow?

If this is all true, why aren't more advisors recommending it for their clients?

What if my client sets up a line of credit, but never uses it?

Many financial inventions have emerged over the history of the world, including pensions, mutual funds, bonds, life insurance, annuities, thirty-year mortgages, etc. Some have passed with no lasting impact, a number were specialized and not easily accessible to the masses, and others are so new that the jury is still out.

Reverse mortgages as we know them are now thirty years old. They have passed the test of time, left a lasting impact, and become easily accessible to the retirement masses. Their most dramatic feature has remained primarily unexplored . . . until now, that is!

> *What if you were told that your client could convert a portion of their home's value into a reserve fund that had a built-in, guaranteed, tax-free minimum growth factor that couldn't be frozen, cancelled, or reduced and could be accessed at any time in the future, regardless of the home's value or your client's income, assets, or credit; what would you say?*

You might say, "Wow!" You may even go back and reread that sentence a few times and say "wow" again. For some, it seems too good to be true. But it is true.

What is this Miracle, Cash-Producing Machine?

What I'm describing is the **Reverse Mortgage Line of Credit**, or what I will commonly call a **ReLOC**.

You will recall that one of the ways a borrower can receive their HECM proceeds is in a line of credit. What is it? Consider a traditional banking line of credit, or even a Visa credit card, but with one significant difference: *the reverse mortgage line of credit (ReLOC) has a built-in, guaranteed growth factor that allows it to grow regardless of the home's value!*

In 2014, I had the opportunity to interview several financial thought leaders at the Center for Retirement Research of Boston College. After they had listened to a lecture on the HECM and its implications for retirement income planning, I asked these leaders, *"What surprised you the most about reverse mortgages?"* The majority emphatically stated, "The line of credit!" They described it as the most powerful, unexpected, and underutilized aspect of the reverse mortgage.

I couldn't agree more. In 2015, I was quoted in *Forbes* magazine as calling the ReLOC the "Swiss Army knife of retirement income planning." I am now more convinced that it could be called the

8th wonder of the world. There is no doubt that the ReLOC is the single most important and accessible retirement income planning tool available today. It's a bold claim, to say the least, but after reading this chapter I think you might agree.

How Much Can a Reverse Mortgage Line of Credit Grow?

Below is a chart showing the growth rate of the ReLOC for a sixty-two-year-old on three different home values. Notice that the unused portion of that line of credit grows automatically at a minimum, guaranteed growth factor.

Note: The interest rates and growth features of the HECM line of credit are adjusted from time to time. These illustrated figures detail a generic ballpark of the program as it exists at the time of this writing.

Year		$200,000 ReLOC Value	$400,000 ReLOC Value	$600,000 ReLOC Value
0		$79,396	$162,796	$248,196
5		$103,118	$211,437	$322,353
10		$133,929	$274,611	$418,668
15		$173,945	$356,661	$543,760
20		$225,917	$463,227	$706,227
25		$309,167	$633,926	$966,472
30		$381,086	$781,391	$1,191,295

How Does It Grow?

For example: a borrower—Age: **70** |Home Value: **$400,000** | Existing Loan Balance: **$100,000**—to display how the line of credit grows.

	Year One
Principal Limit (PL)	$200,000
Outstanding Balance (OB)	$115,000
Available Line of Credit (LOC)	$85,000

- The initial ReLOC amounts are based on the age of the youngest borrower (70), the home's value ($400,000), and current interest rates. In this example, the reverse mortgage makes $200,000 available. This is called the PRINCIPAL LIMIT (PL).

- Since a reverse mortgage must be a first mortgage, the borrower's existing mortgage of $100,000 is paid off. There were closing costs of $15,000 financed into the loan. Therefore, the beginning OUTSTANDING BALANCE (OB) is $115,0000 ($100,000 + $15,000 = $115,000).

- When we subtract the outstanding balance (OB) from the principal limit (PL), we get the LINE OF CREDIT (LOC) amount of $85,000 ($200,000 - $115,000 = $85,000).

How the Balance Grows Over Time

	Year One	Year Two
Principal Limit	$200,000	$210,000
Outstanding Balance	$115,000	$120,250
Available Line of Credit	$85,000	$89,750

- Over the first year, the **principal limit (PL)** continues to grow at the outstanding **effective interest rate** at the time (we are using 5%). You will notice that it's grown to **$210,000.** *This rate is calculated by adding the loan index plus the lender's margin plus HUD's mortgage insurance premium charge* of 0.5 percent. *The effective interest rate is the note rate of 0.5 percent.*

- The outstanding balance (OB), or what your client owes, grows at the same rate. It's now $120,250.

- Therefore, the line of credit has grown as well. By subtracting the outstanding balance (OB) from the principal limit (PL), you'll find the ReLOC is now $89,750 ($210,000 - $120,250 = $89,750).

Pretty simple so far, right? The principal limit and the outstanding balance continue to grow at the same rate, resulting in the growth of the available line of credit.

Growth in Excess of $282,000

	Yr. 1	Yr. 2	Yr. 10	Yr. 15
Principal Limit	$200,000	$210,000	$325,799	$415,786
Outstanding Balance	$115,000	$120,250	$187,323	$239,077
Line of Credit	$85,000	$89,750	$138,476	$176,709

	Yr. 20	Yr. 25	Yr. 30	
Principal Limit	$530,660	$677,271	$864,388	
Outstanding Balance	$305,129	$389,431	$497,023	
Line of Credit	$225,531	$287,840	$367,365	

Each year, the line of credit will continue to replenish itself by subtracting the current outstanding balance from the current principal limit. The chart shows the growth of the ReLOC assuming no withdrawals are taken. It begins with $85,000 and thirty years later has grown to over $367,000.

Can you see the value to your client of having access to the appreciating line of credit? How much will they appreciate *you* for having helped them unlock their home's equity?

Appreciating Home Value

Don't forget what else is growing as well: the **home's value**. Below is a chart that shows the initial home value of $400,000 growing at 4 percent (the historic home appreciation average) on the top row and 2 percent on the bottom.

	Yr.10	Yr.15	Yr.20	Yr.25	Yr.30
Home Value (4%)	$592,000	$720,000	$877,000	$1,066,000	$1,297,000
Home Value (2%)	$488,000	$538,000	$594,000	$656,000	$725,000

Six Key Features of the ReLOC

I am out of breath from the excitement of what this means for you and your clients! Clearly, the reverse mortgage line of credit is in a league of its own. It is one of the most foundational, accessible, and versatile retirement income planning tools available today. Here's a summary of its six key features:

- **Reliability:** Cannot be frozen, cancelled, or reduced. It can be used at any time for any reason, without anything catastrophic having occurred. Client has access to dollars regardless of their personal income, assets, or credit scores.

- **Flexibility**: No required payments when funds are accessed. No ongoing premiums, spikes, or increases. It's bidirectional, meaning dollars can be repaid and accessed later if needed.

- **Taxability**: Proceeds and growth are non-taxable.

- **Expandability**: Growth is guaranteed for as long as the line of credit is open and independent of home value.

- **Affordability**: A one-time out-of-pocket cost of $500 unlocks your clients' access to their home's equity.

- **Insurability**: Even if all the funds are drawn upon and the balance owed ends up being more than the home is worth at time of repayment, FHA ensures that neither the home-owner, heirs or estate has any personal responsibility to repay the remaining balance after home sale proceeds. No deficiency judgment will be taken against the heirs or estate.

How is a ReLOC different than a HELOC?

I think you now know the answer to this question, but a study conducted in March of 2017 by the National Council on Aging may shed some light on how your clients perceive the difference. The study asked several focus groups, comprised of leading-edge boomers and existing retirees, to choose the loan that best suited them.

Study One: The first study asked the group if they would prefer a reverse mortgage or a traditional home equity line of credit without providing any details other than the names. The clear majority chose the home equity line of credit.

Study Two: Then they brought in a new group and described the features of the two types of loans—this time *without giving product names* (see chart below). When asked which loan they would prefer, the group overwhelmingly chose product B. Can you tell which one it is?

More groups were brought in and more experiments conducted. They discovered that most retirees were overwhelmingly in favor of the HECM line of credit benefits (product B) but *held a bias against the term "reverse mortgage"!*

Consider Using the Terms Home Equity, Housing Wealth, or HECMs.

The Most Important Insurance a Retiree Can Have?

Do you know the most important insurance a retiree can have? Simple: it's **Equity Insurance**.

Equity Insurance is access to the appreciating equity in a client's home regardless of the home's future value. **We're talking about access that cannot be frozen, cancelled, or reduced; is not dependent on the client's income or assets; and has** dollars growing and coming out tax-free! There is no doubt in my mind that equity insurance should be part of every retirement income planning conversation.

Product Name Experiment

Key Product Features

Please assume that the total costs and fees for both products are about the same. Both A and B are line of credit products for accessing a homeowner's home equity to meet expenses.

Loan Type A	Loan Type B
Access to the line for ten years	No mandatory ten-year draw
Must make minimum monthly payments	No minimum payments required
Lender can freeze or cancel loan amounts	Lender cannot freeze or cancel loan amounts
Home subject to foreclosure if minimum payments, taxes and insurance are not paid	Home subject to foreclosure if taxes and insurance are not paid
Loan balance must be paid back in full, even if the borrower owes more than the home is worth	Borrowers or heirs never pay back more than home's fair market value when sold

Most of your clients are already paying for homeowners' insurance. I've been paying a premium since I bought my first home in 1994! However, the probability of using those insurance policies and recouping their investment is low in many cases. The chart below will allow me to put this into perspective.

Insurance Type	Annual Cost	Retirement Out-of-Pocket Costs	Lost Opportunity Costs	Probability of Major Use
Homeowners	$1,000	$30,000	$80,000	2-3%
Auto	$2,000	$60,000	$160,000	16.5%
	$3,000	$90,000	$240,000	
Equity Insurance	$500	$500	$800,000	50-75%

The national average for homeowners' insurance is $1,000 per year. If you multiply this over a projected thirty-year retirement (not to mention what was spent during their working years), your clients are reasonably expected to have spent an additional $30,000. However, the probability that the retired clients (over age sixty-five) will have a major use of the insurance is very small, as you can see in the chart. If the clients were able to invest those same dollars at a reasonable rate of return, they would have added $80,000 to their portfolio.

Auto insurance on two cars averages about $2,000 per year, and you can see what happens over a thirty-year retirement (not accounting for inflation). With each of those insurances, the client has spent real dollars, and the only way to get a return is if something calamitous happens.

Notice, however, that the equity insurance on a $400,000 home is very different (see earlier chart of $400k ReLOC). The out-of-pocket cost to obtain equity insurance is around $500. Unlike the other insurances, this one does not require any ongoing "premium payments." Meanwhile, the potential lost-opportunity costs soar to an average of $800,000. See the difference?

With equity insurance, the client can establish a growing reserve of dollars that will be accessible to them for as long as they have the loan, independent of the home's value. They can use the funds and pay them back to free those dollars up again, or they can access them and not have the burden of a monthly repayment. The choice is theirs, but the reality is that the probability of your clients needing those dollars over a long retirement is very high.

Question: What is the value to your clients' retirement outcomes and peace of mind to have a back-up plan for risk, volatility, and the "what ifs" in life?

What if you told your client that they could convert a portion of their home's value into a reserve fund that had a built-in, guaranteed, tax-free minimum growth factor that couldn't be frozen, cancelled, or reduced and could be accessed at any time in the future, regardless of their home's value or their income, assets, or credit? What would they say?

The studies mentioned earlier suggest they would certainly want to hear about it. The HECM line of credit may be the most underutilized aspect of the reverse mortgage, but it could win awards for potential. Hopefully, before you finish this book, you will begin to grasp its tremendous value in retirement income planning.

7

Bridging the Gap

The HECM Term or Tenure Payment

I heard that a reverse mortgage can pay my clients monthly for the duration of the loan, but what if they only need payments for a limited time?

I'm concerned that the dollars my clients receive from the reverse mortgage will affect their adjusted gross income as well as be a tax liability, is this true?

Upon retiring, most seniors rely on fixed monthly income to meet their living essentials. They are comfortable with this. In an earlier chapter, I mentioned that one of the ways HECM proceeds can be received is on a monthly basis; structuring the reverse mortgage this way can fit very well into an established retirement budget and plan.

There are two types of monthly payments available:

- **Tenure Payments**: Money is received for as long as the clients have the loan open and meet the conditions outlined in the earlier chapter (*maintain home, pay taxes and insurance*).

- **Term Payments:** Clients choose to receive a specific monthly payment for a fixed amount of time and this amount can be adjusted as needed.

Both monthly payment calculations are based on the age and life expectancy of the youngest borrower at time of selection.

Understanding the Conversion for a Tenure Payment

Once a HECM is initiated and the initial line of credit amount is determined, the clients may choose the **tenure or term payment** option. In the chart below, you will see an illustration of the initial line of credit and monthly tenure payment amounts based on three different home values. However, the real power of this tool is that your client can choose to allow the line of credit to grow and at any point in the future, they may convert their existing line of credit into higher monthly tenure payments.

Estimated Home Values

Yr	Age	$200,000 Line of Credit	$200,000 Monthly Payment	$400,000 Line of Credit	$400,000 Monthly Payment	$600,000 Line of Credit	$600,000 Monthly Payment
0	65	$79,396	$430	$162,796	$869	$248,196	$1,324
5	70	$103,118	$587	$211,437	$1,185	$322,353	$1,805
10	75	$133,929	$828	$274,611	$1,673	$418,668	$2,548
15	80	$173,945	$1,207	$356,661	$2,439	$543,760	$3,715
20	85	$225,917	$1,885	$463,227	$3,747	$706,227	$5,708
25	90	$309,167	$3,141	$633,926	$6,344	$966,472	$9,664
30	95	$404,434	$6,662	$830,952	$13,456	$1,265,870	$20,497

Bridging the Gap with a Term Payment

What if your clients do not want or need a monthly payment for an indefinite amount of time? What if they only need income for a 3, 5 or 8-year period of time? This is where the HECM Term payment may make sense.

Let's consider why a person may only need money for a short period of time. Below is a list of common uses of the term payment option.

- **Social Security Deferral**: Clients' retirement plans call for them to defer Social Security until age 70, but something has happened, and they need income now. Converting the HECM Line of Credit into a monthly payment to cover the gap from their current age until their optimized Social Security withdrawal age could work well.

- **Gap Healthcare:** A client has left the workforce at age 62 and doesn't have healthcare coverage for the next three years until eligible for Medicaid. The term payment can be used to pay for COBRA, or another healthcare provider, until that time.

- **Qualified Plan Deferral:** The term payment allows clients to keep the full value of their investments working as long as possible before taking distributions.

- **Annuity Deferral for Vesting**: Many annuities contractually guarantee a greater annuitized payout, if clients can keep the funds in the plan longer (vesting). If funds are needed sooner, they could simply use the HECM Term payment while the annuities grow and then turn it off when they annuitize at a higher payout rate.

- **Tax Bracket Management**: Sometimes clients may be on the fence between two tax brackets and drawing money from certain investments will push them into the higher bracket—potentially costing them thousands of dollars, or even causing their Social Security benefits to be taxed. Since the proceeds of the HECM are not taxable, clients could use the HECM Term payment to live on, thus, keeping them within a lower Modified Adjusted Gross Income and tax bracket!

These are just a few ideas on how converting the line of credit into a monthly tenure or term payments can enhance retirement outcomes, others will be presented in later chapters.

8

Is There an Optimal Time to Establish a ReLOC?

My understanding is that FINRA and other scholars advocate using reverse mortgages as a last resort. Has something changed?

I have been reading lately that setting up a reverse mortgage line of credit earlier rather than later is preferable; for what reason?

I f you knew that your clients were planning to stay in their home for the foreseeable future and were interested in accessing the appreciating equity in their homes (at any time and for any reason), how early in retirement would you suggest they establish a HECM line of credit?

This was the question that began to emerge in 2012 as many financial thought leaders took notice of the power and versatility of the reverse mortgage line of credit.

The Compelling Research that Helped Change FINRA's Position

One notable research paper, "Reversing the Conventional Wisdom: Using Home Equity to Supplement Retirement Income"

(Barry H. Sacks, J.D., Ph.D. and Stephen R. Sacks, Ph.D.), took to task the seminal notion that using reverse mortgages as a last resort was best. The writers discovered that the prevailing position, popularized by the Financial Industry Regulatory Authority (FINRA), stating that HECMs should only be established after the portfolio was nearly exhausted, was not correct.

What the math and science showed was:

> "If you use the reverse mortgage credit line in a coordinated fashion—meaning timing it so that it just fills in the down parts of the volatility cycle of the securities portfolio, the portfolio lasts much longer, and most important for any retiree, the cash flow survives much longer. It survives so much longer that in many cases, it doubles the probability that the cash flow will last as long as the retiree does." **– Dr. Barry Sacks**

The research-based argument was so powerful that in October 2013 it led FINRA to change its "reverse mortgage as a last resort" position.

Their research showed that if the HECM line of credit functions in the way described, then it is best to establish one sooner rather than later. As a matter of fact, several scholars have suggested *setting it up at the onset of retirement* because the earlier it is established, the more time it has to grow and the more funds the borrowers will have access to. This just makes sense, in my opinion, but it's great to have the research to solidify it.

Furthermore, Dr. Wade Pfau's 2016 book, *Reverse Mortgages: How to Use Reverse Mortgages to Secure Your Retirement*, went even further than others by not just stating the best time to set up a ReLOC, but showing how an earlier versus later strategy fared. He explored different methods for incorporating home equity into a retirement income plan using a reverse mortgage.

In the following chart, Dr. Pfau graphically shows the value of establishing a HECM line of credit sooner rather than later.

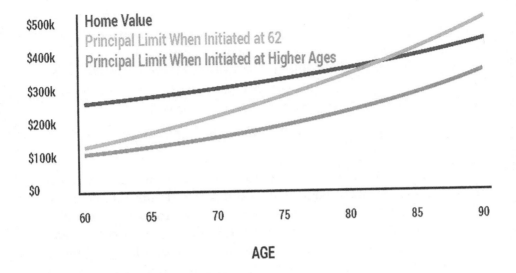

- The top line shows the value of the home appreciating over time.

- The middle line shows a retiree establishing a ReLOC at the onset of retirement and allowing it to grow.

- The bottom line shows a client waiting to establish a ReLOC until later in retirement. In theory, by doing this the loan benefit would be greater because the client is older, and the home is worth more, but as the chart shows, the odds that the delayed line would catch up with the earlier are pretty slim.

7 Ways to Incorporate Housing Wealth with a Million Dollar Client

Next, Dr. Pfau incorporated research that told a compelling story involving a retiree with $1 million in tax-deferred retirement assets, a home valued at $500,000, and 4 percent (or $40,000) in needed retirement cash flow. A 25 percent marginal tax bracket was assumed, and the homeowner's cash needs were adjusted each year for inflation. The research used a Monte Carlo simulator 10,000 times and demonstrated the best and worst possible outcomes. Below is an explanation of the findings.

The lowest two lines explained:

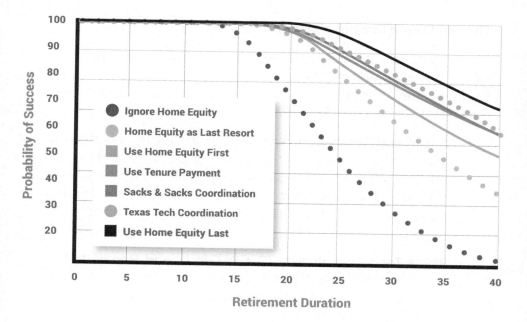

- **Ignore/Never Use**: The bottom line (dotted) shows those who didn't use a HECM at all—ever! This option yielded a 39 percent probability of success at the thirty-year mark.

- **Last Resort**: The second line from the bottom (dotted), representing those who established a reverse mortgage only *after* the savings ran out, yielded a 69 percent probability of success at the thirty-year mark.

The next best two lines explained:

- **Use First**: The third line from the bottom (solid) shows those who established a HECM at the *onset* of retirement and use it *first* instead of other savings, and then they used other savings after it ran out. It revealed a 75 percent probability of success.

- **Use Tenure**: The fourth line from the bottom (solid) shows those who established a HECM at the onset of retirement and converted it into a **monthly payment**. This allowed them to draw less from their savings and thus preserve them longer. It showed an 80 percent probability of success.

The final three lines explained:

All three of the strategies below are based on establishing the HECM line of credit at the onset of retirement and allowing it to grow. The differences between them are regarding when and how exactly to use the ReLOC.

- **Sacks and Sacks Coordination/Set it, Get It, and Keep It**: The third line from the top (solid) showed setting up the ReLOC and using it versus the savings during a bear market with the proceeds not being repaid. This method, favored by Dr. Barry Sacks and Dr. Stephen Sacks, produced an 81 percent success probability.

- **Texas Tech Coordination/Set It, Get It, and Repay It:** This strategy, shown by the second line from the top (dotted), is similar to Sacks and Sacks, but says that you should use the HECM as income during bear markets and *repay* during bulls. This method was preferred by the Harold Evensky, CFP—Texas Tech Team and gave an 82 percent success probability.

- **Use Home Equity Last/Set It and Forget It**: Represented by the solid top line, this strategy says to set up the HECM line of credit and allow it to grow, but only use it after the savings are exhausted. This, in theory, would have allowed it to grow exponentially over that time. Dr. Pfau found that opening the HECM line of credit at the start of retirement and then delaying its use until the portfolio is depleted creates downside protection for the retirement income plan. The result was a nearly 90 percent probability of success at the thirty-year mark.

All three of these final research strategies allow the line of credit to grow larger, perhaps even surpassing the home's value. This provides a substantially larger reserve fund to draw from should the portfolio be prematurely depleted. The differences in the outcomes were negligible between the three, but the key theme remained: *there is great value for clients to open a reverse mortgage line of credit as early as possible.*

Some financial planners will begrudgingly agree to use home equity as a last resort, but as you can see, that has the second-worst outcome. If the client's primary concern is running out of money and the planner consistently recommends the option with the lowest chance of portfolio survival, then they may not be acting in the best interest of the client.

Mini Case Study: A Word from the Dean

To illustrate the ease in which these principles can be incorporated into your retirement planning conversations, here's a word from venerated author and the "Dean" of financial planning, Dr. Harold Evensky. In July of 2012, he delivered the keynote address on retirement planning at a summit held at the Wharton School of the University of Pennsylvania. To everyone's surprise, he concluded his presentation by speaking about how reverse mortgages, particularly the line of credit and its financial planning implications, had really surprised him.

> *"I see the reverse mortgage as a risk management tool—not as leverage, not as credit, not as cash flow. It's unlike a home equity loan; it is non-cancelable, which is what happened during the grand recession. They got canceled. We go from a two-bucket approach to a three-bucket approach, so if we ever get to the point where we can cut down that second bucket from two years to six months—and if we ever use that up—then we would tap into this reverse mortgage. The markets get better; we pay it back again."*—**Dr. Harold Evensky**

Evensky's premise was stunning in its simplicity and conversational brilliance. Instead of keeping emergency dollars in reserve where they are not growing, use the ReLOC as the emergency fund and repurpose those reserve funds for better growth. Now, that was easy!

Repurposed Reserve Strategy

All Investments	24 – 36 Month Reserve	ReLOC
4% - 12% Growth	0% - 1% Growth	4% - 10% Growth

9

Are Reverse Mortgages Expensive?

I hear closing costs for reverse mortgages are expensive. How are the costs of the reverse mortgage calculated?

How would I determine if the costs of the reverse mortgage are worth having my client pursue it?

" Don, are the closing costs on this reverse mortgage really $16,000? Please advise!"

Over the last twenty years, I have fielded this email, phone call, or reaction many times over. The single biggest concern I encounter from informed advisors (those who have begun to embrace reverse mortgages) is this question of costs. It's such an important subject that I wanted to commit an entire chapter to unpacking it.

What Are the Costs to Establish a Reverse Mortgage?

Like many other types of loans, there are costs associated with obtaining a HECM. Below is a description and a chart outlining the standard acquisition cost for a HECM today. It shows different home values and the three cost categories.

- **FHA Mortgage Insurance Premiums.** This required insurance is purchased by the borrower and financed into the loan. It goes to the Federal Housing Administration (a division of the United States Department of Housing and Urban Development—HUD), and guarantees that *the total debt repayment will never be greater than the value of the home* at the time of repayment.

  It also guarantees that you will receive your promised loan advances and will not have to repay the loan for as long as you live in the home and meet the requirements of the loan. It is currently calculated at 2 percent of the home's appraised value (up to the lending limit).

- **Loan Origination Fee**. The lender is permitted to charge a fee to cover their costs. HUD sets the maximum amount to be calculated at 2 percent of the first $200,000 of the home's value and 1 percent of any remaining value. The maximum amount that can be charged is $6,000.

- **Third-Party Fees.** This includes costs charged by third-party vendors associated with transacting and closing the loan, such as title insurance, appraisal, credit report, settlement fee, endorsements, counseling, flood/tax certificate, and a notary. These charges typically range between 0.5 percent to 1 percent of the home's appraised value (up to the lending limit). Most of these fees (with the exception of the appraisal) can usually be financed into the loan.

HECM Acquisition Costs

Description/Purpose	Home Values		
	$200,000	$400,000	$600,000
Mortgage Insurance Premium	$4,000	$8,000	$12,000
Lender Origination	$4,000	$6,000	$6,000
Third-Party Charges	$1,000	$2,000	$3,000
	$9,000	$16,000	$21,000

It's important to understand that the market changes, and sometimes lenders can issue credits when certain factors are in place, but that doesn't always happen. After finishing this chapter, you may discover that these credits, though helpful when available, may not be a determining factor as much as you might think.

Do the Costs of a Reverse Mortgage Make Sense for Your Clients?

Undoubtedly, a fair question, and the truth is that a HECM *may not make sense for your clients!*

I have now had over 20,000 consumer/advisor-facing conversations that have led to nearly 3,000 reverse mortgage clients. All that tells you is that as good as reverse mortgages are for many, they're not always the best thing to do. However, out of all the people who chose not to pursue a HECM (either by their choice or my suggestion), only a handful had issues concerning the pricing.

Everyone knows that all financial products, services, or strategies have a cost associated with them, and reverse mortgages are no different.

In my time in this business, I have seen the closing costs of reverse mortgages range from $125 to $25,000 or more. The federal government (through HUD), as the program's custodian, makes periodic changes that can cause pricing vacillations, and the secondary market (which subsequently purchases the loans) has pricing influence as well. This will not change; therefore, HECM pricing, like that of every other product, will continue to ebb and flow.

Four Questions that Are More Important than Price

Back to the advisor's original concern: are reverse mortgages expensive, and do the costs make sense for my clients?

The truth is that it doesn't matter what the pricing of reverse mortgages are *right now*, as that will fluctuate. There are four other and more significant questions to consider before price. When weighing the reverse mortgage options, simply ask:

1. What problem does it solve?

2. What risk does it insure?

3. What expense will they have?

4. What alternative works better?

Question 1: What Problem Does It Solve?

Are reverse mortgages expensive?

"Compared to what?" is my usual response. Before I can assess the "value" of a product or service, I first need to know what it is and what it does.

Let me share a story with you that will provide a framework for my response.

The University of Kentucky basketball program had gotten a reputation for recruiting superstar high school players who spent one year in college and then declared for the NBA draft. Kentucky had done it yet again: they recruited a young man named Steve who was a mixture of Lebron James and Michael Jordan, just better!

Right before NCAA finals, Steve noticed his right eye was a little blurry in the mornings. A few days later, both eyes were blurry. It wasn't too bad—just a nuisance—but before the week's end, he was really struggling to see and suspected something was seriously wrong.

He told his coaches and team doctors. They called in his parents and flew him to the best vision specialist in the country. After a few hours and several tests, the results came in.

"Steve, we have good news and bad news," said the doctor.

"What is the bad news, doc?"

"The bad news," said the doctor, "is you have a very rare condition that is causing an accelerated blindness in both eyes. Unfortunately, in two to three weeks, you will be totally and irreversibly blind."

Alarmed and filled with tears, his mother asked, "What could possibly be the good news?"

The doctor replied, "Oh, the good news is that it's 100 percent treatable with a 99.9 percent success rate because we caught it early. Recovery should last about two weeks, and you won't have to worry about this issue ever coming back again."

Huge relief swept over the room. There were tears of joy, hugs and a sigh of relief from Steve's agent. Then, from the corner, the voice of his father said, "Can I ask a question?"

"Of course," the doctor replied.

"How much will this cost?"

Stunned with disbelief, the doctor answered, "His eyesight."

The father's question, given the circumstances, was absurd, because the *price* of the procedure was not the same as the *cost* to the patient. The "cost" was the irreversible loss of his vision in both eyes and the subsequent financial loss of not playing in the NBA. **Cost is always different from price.**

When someone says, "Reverse mortgages are expensive," we must ask, "Compared to what?" You see, the real answer lies in the question, *what is the financial problem that the reverse mortgage is solving?* Or better stated: *What is the cost of NOT doing the HECM?*

It's hard to determine the cost of a financial solution until you know the problem it is solving. In an earlier chapter, I spoke about the importance of centering the conversation around the client's five core concerns: **Longevity, Lifestyle, Liquidity, Legacy, and Long-Term Care**. Starting here is critical because it allows the client to self-diagnose and articulate their comfort or pain levels.

If a HECM strategy is not solving a problem, or if there is a better resolution, then it may not be the right solution for your clients, and the costs of acquisition may not be justified. If it does solve the problem and is the best alternative, given the others mentioned, then the "costs" are not relevant.

Question 2: What Risk Does It Insure?

Earlier, I stated that every financial decision has both a price and cost associated with it. For example, what is the cost of your clients *not* having homeowner's insurance when something serious happens? What is the consequence? Simple: they carry the sole risk of paying the cost of damage. It's called **Liability Transfer Risk**.

Most people do not purchase insurance because they want to use it, but because they don't want to bear the personal financial responsibility of not being covered.

There are times in life when we make a choice to shoulder an expense now to insure against something that may or may not happen in the future. Other examples include:

- When the doctor said the growth was not cancerous but could develop into something later in life and suggests that you do surgery and/or a treatment protocol just to be safe.

- When you choose to move to a different (more expensive) neighborhood to get your kids into different schools so that they will have an educational advantage.

- When the car dealer says that you might want to consider the extended warranty just in case.

- When your advisor says you should have six to twenty-four months of cash reserve just in case.

We are all accustomed to making daily decisions about the risks of life and whether we want to bear the financial responsibility if something goes sideways. We choose to pay for insurance ahead of time just in case it does.

I have already mentioned the eighteen major possibilities that your clients' retirement income could go sideways. Most clients are concerned about such worries as not having enough savings to last all of retirement (or low interest rates eroding savings), risk, volatility, inflation, the increasing costs of health care, the tenuousness of pensions, and the uncertainty of Social Security.

The real question is, are they prepared for those risks and willing to take the financial responsibility if the outcomes don't go as expected? Are you willing to release them into retirement without a viable back-up plan to insure those risks?

As you will see in the case studies, establishing a HECM, particularly the line of credit, is a proven, powerful, and viable way to help your clients insure against some of the major risks in retirement. The subsequent question becomes: **Is insuring their retirement risks worth the acquisition costs of setting up a HECM?**

> **"What is the value of having your retirement insured?"**
>
> **"What is the risk of not having it insured?"**
>
> **Have you had conversations with your clients about insuring their retirement income?**

Question 3: What Expense Will They Have?

After the glare the husband received from his wife, the young athlete's father signed the papers then and there. To his great relief, their excellent insurance plan ended up covering 98 percent of the surgery and recovery costs.

In the story, who ends up bearing the burden of the "cost" of the surgery? It was the insurance company. When establishing a HECM and looking at the closing costs, what is the client actually paying out of their own pockets? Usually $300 to $500; the house pays the rest!

An advisor recently asked me to speak to one of his clients who was having trouble swallowing a $16,000 closing cost. Here is my conversation:

DG: How much did you pay for this house when you bought it?

CL: We paid $17,500, but that was forty years ago.

DG: Was that a lot of money at the time?

CL: It was back then; we could barely afford it.

DG: Tell me the truth, in your wildest imagination, did you ever think that your house would be worth $400,000, more than twenty times what you paid for it?

CL: Never. We couldn't even count that high forty years ago.

DG: It would be like telling some young couple today that their $400,000 home will one day be worth $8 million and they would still be living in it . . . crazy, right, but it happened to you!

CL: It is crazy, but you're right; we're living proof that it can happen.

DG: Let me ask you a question: what did you do differently from your neighbors that caused your house value to increase from $17,500 to $400,000?

CL: Well, we put in a new kitchen and siding, but I guess all our neighbors did similarly. I suppose that we didn't really do anything that others didn't do, too. The house and the whole neighborhood all grew in value over the years.

DG: Exactly, the house did that all on its own. So, since you had nothing to do with the growth, let me ask you a question: **Would it be okay for the house to give back $16,000 of that growth to create the financial peace of mind and retirement outcomes you have worked hard for?**

They got it. The house is paying for it! When I told them their out-of-pocket expense was only going to be $500, they really understood!

An Example from a Mentor

When I first began in this business, I was fortunate to become friends with Monte Rose, who was a "HECM giant." Up to that point in time, he had done the single largest reverse mortgage loan in history (in excess of $15 million).

When one of his clients was concerned about the closing costs of the loan, Monte would ask, "How much is it worth for you to secure your retirement peace of mind?"

Then, taking their closing costs ($16,000), he would divide that by the number of years they thought they would stay in the home (18 years). He then divided that by the number of days in a year (365). He would then rephrase the question: *"Is your retirement peace of mind worth $2.50 a day?"*

What a great question! This logic is further strengthened by the fact that the clients themselves are *not* paying the $2.50. The house is.

That's the main idea. The closing costs of a reverse mortgage are borne by the house itself and will be repaid by the house, while the actual out-of-pocket financial impact to the client is negligible.

Question 4: What Alternative Works Better?

I hope I've been clear that I do not believe that a reverse mortgage is always the best option. However, as we are examining the "cost," we must include this last question: given the options available, does your client have a better alternative to meet their retirement income objectives?

Over the last two decades, I have had clients provide eight alternatives. Having an in-depth conversation about these alternatives is primarily the job of your qualified HECM partner. Yet, it's still very important for the advisor to understand each alternative.

Let's briefly explore each.

- **Sell and Move:** This is always my first suggested consideration because it is often the most effective alternative for a successful retirement. After navigating the emotional issues attached to a house, I will ask, "Mr. and Mrs. Montini, *are you open* to moving to a different home, if it could enhance your retirement?" (See Chapter 15)

- **Cash in Other Resources**: Sometimes clients have savings, investments, or permanent life insurance from which they're willing to draw, or they may consider selling or borrowing on a second home to solve the financial challenge. Advisors must help their clients weigh the benefits of using all or some of these other resources to meet the need.

Helping a Son Not Lose His Business

An advisor's client had a son whose business had a $100,000 tax penalty that the son couldn't pay. The son was in danger of losing his business and home. The client had $400,000 in savings and thought she could easily draw from those funds and lend them to her son. She spoke to her advisor about helping her son, and he affirmed her desire to offer aid. He suggested that she consider all of her available assets. Which source could help her accomplish her goal without severely impacting savings? She also needed to consider the taxes she would need to pay (*she forgot about taxes being owed on the money she would take out*). After doing the math with her advisor, she decided that unlocking her home equity with a HECM reverse mortgage was the best option. It was tax free, did not deplete her savings, and could be replenished little by little as her son paid her back.

- **Borrow Money from Family**: I have found that most children are willing to help their parents, but often are not prepared to provide the amount of money their parents may need up-front or over time for an extended retirement. Furthermore, the clients are usually uncomfortable asking their children for this type of help. Having a sense of dignity and independence is important to them. At this juncture, you might ask, *"Would you be comfortable having your children assist you with your retirement income needs?"*

- **Refinance**: Recent studies tell us a large portion of baby boomers will be carrying housing debt into retirement. A simple strategy for them to consider is refinancing into a lower payment. This is a good choice for many, but for others, it does not solve the cash flow or savings erosion problems. The difficulties may be lessened, but the ultimate problem may still persist.

- **Find a Roommate**: Renting out a spare room or finding a senior roommate can often be a good solution. It provides income and companionship when it works well.

- **Research Local Programs:** Some retirees may be eligible for local programs that provide essentials. Cash and food assistance, along with home repair or weatherization, are often available to clients who meet the income requirements.

- **Go Back to Work:** Retirees have mixed reactions to this. Some say they'd like to, but no one will hire them. Others say, "Not on your life." Most are somewhere in between. Regardless of their reaction, part-time work is often a great retirement income supplement.

- **Do Nothing/Wait:** Sometimes waiting or not doing anything is the most appropriate thing to do. My experience has taught me that in most cases, by the time the HECM conversation comes up, the situation has worsened. I will often ask, *"If you don't make some changes, do you think things will get better or worse?"*

"Is there any alternative that I have missed?" is the concluding question I typically ask advisors and clients. I have discovered that this list encompasses almost everything.

Back to the Question at Hand

So, how would I justify a $16,000 financed closing cost for a reverse mortgage? I wouldn't, but what I would do is honestly reflect, work through the four questions and see where we arrive.

What problem does it solve? Does a HECM help resolve the clients' Longevity, Lifestyle, Liquidity, Legacy, or Long-Term Care concerns? If we don't implement a HECM strategy at this time, will the problem stay the same, get better, or get worse?

What risk does it insure? I would make sure the client understood the risks associated with retirement income and felt comfortable with the potential risks of insuring their own retirement. I'd even give them a disclosure document stating that you discussed the risks to retirement and presented housing wealth as a possible insuring alternative (Chapter 19).

What expense will they have? I would confirm the client understood that they're only paying a one-time, $300 to $500, out-of-pocket cost and that the house is paying all remaining closing costs.

What alternative works better? Your client always has a choice, even if that choice isn't one that you believe is financially prudent. My final question to clients and their advisors is very simple: "*Is the reverse mortgage the absolutely best alternative to address your financial concerns given everything we have discussed?*" If the answer is yes, then we proceed to help the client. If it's no, you help them choose the best path to achieve their retirement outcomes.

It's pretty straightforward. Understanding these concepts will not lessen the price of a HECM and certainly will not prove that they are a good idea for your client, but it will allow you to put the "costs" into the correct perspective.

So, the next time you hear a person say, "Reverse mortgages are expensive," be sure to filter your response through the four questions:

- **What problem will it solve?**
- **What risk will it insure?**
- **What expense will they have?**
- **What alternative works better?**

SECTION 3:

CASE STUDIES AND CONVERSATION GUIDES:

Practical Strategies For Introducing Housing Wealth To Your Clients

How do I talk to my clients about reverse mortgages? What can I share? When do I share it? How do I share it? That is the question that has been a stumbling block to many. (Remember the advisor from chapter five?)

In this section, we will share the practical guidelines to answer those questions. We'll expand on the second way and **introduce** the third way reverses mortgages have changed the retirement income conversation.

1. Reverse mortgages have changed the way advisors **SEE** the housing asset.

2. Reverse mortgages have changed the way advisors **SOLVE** the five most pressing retirement concerns.

3. Reverse mortgages have changed the way advisors **SEAMLESSLY** incorporate housing wealth into planning.

What You Will Discover in This Section:

- HECM-focused, retirement income case studies centered on the five core boomer concerns: Longevity, Lifestyle, Liquidity, Legacy, and Long-Term Care.

- How the strategic uses of reverse mortgages can cover several concerns simultaneously.

- Case studies, each of which includes: Client Overview | Planning Objective | Financial Profile | Available Housing Wealth Opportunities | Primary Concern Addressed.

- Very simple questions and conversation starters that will help you introduce the subject.

The 5 L's

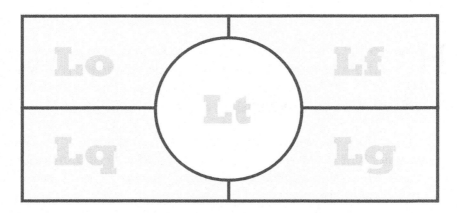

Case Studies and Conversation Guides

Case Studies and Conversation Guides	5 Core Concerns				
	Lo	Lf	Lq	Lg	Lt
Mitigating Risks and Increasing Longevity with the HECM	√	√		√	
Paychecks and Playchecks Re-Imagined: Creating Longevity for Risk-Averse Clients	√	√			
The HECM Replacement: The Power of Eliminating a Mortgage Payment	√	√			
Expanding Your Planning Possibilities: Thank Heaven for 7-11		√	√		
The HECM Exchange: The Power of Keeping a Mortgage Payment			√		√
Using the HECM for Purchase to Add $226,000 to Clients' Savings			√	√	√
How to Free Money for Clients to Achieve Legacy Both Now and Later				√	
Social Security Optimization	√	√			
Gray Divorce		√	√		
Mini Case Studies Previously Discussed					
"The Rule of 30" vs. "The 4% Rule"	√				
Repurposed Reserve Strategy	√	√			
How Housing Wealth Can Help Client without Using HECM Proceeds		√		√	

10

How the HECM Can Significantly Increase Savings Success Rates

> *"Retirement is like a long vacation in Las Vegas. The goal is to enjoy it the fullest, but not so fully that you run out of money."*
>
> **– Jonathan Clements**

An advisor's energy and clients' concerns are focused on ensuring there are enough assets that can be converted to income to meet their basic retirement expenses for the duration of their retirement (Longevity). In the next two chapters, we will look at two case studies that show how the HECM can address the longevity conversation.

The first study is particularly relevant to advisors with wealth management practices, while the other is geared toward annuity/life insurance-focused practices. The case studies are not a commentary on which planning strategy works best but rather on how the HECM seamlessly integrates into both. The goal is to show how adding housing wealth to the longevity conversation can have long lasting impact for the advisor, their clients, and the clients' estate.

There are many factors that impact longevity, some of which are within the control of the client and others which are not. For example, excessive withdrawals from the account are in the client's control, but inflation, volatility, and sequence risks are not. Before we move to applying the HECM, we must first take a quick look at those three challenges.

Three Mandatory Considerations for a Modern Retirement Income Plan

Inflation simply means products and goods are more expensive over time. Technically speaking, it is the rate at which the general level of prices for goods and services is rising and, as a result, the rate at which the purchasing power of money is falling.

The historic average for inflation since 1914 is 3.25 percent, but let's say, for example, the inflation rate is 4 percent. In that case, a jacket that costs $100 today will cost $104 next year and $180 in fifteen years.

Years	Inflation Rate - $100			
	3%	4%	5%	6%
10	$134	$148	$163	$179
15	$156	$180	$208	$240
20	$181	$219	$265	$321
25	$209	$267	$339	$429
30	$243	$324	$432	$574

Obviously, this can have a devastating effect on retirement. When inflation rates are high, a retiree's savings don't go as far, and this can significantly impact the survival rate of the retiree's portfolio. As rates increase, more money must be pulled from the portfolio, eroding it more quickly. A modern retirement income plan MUST account for inflation.

Volatility: It is well known that the value of a portfolio goes up and down based on market performance. Consider the impact of an investor losing 50 percent on a $100 investment in one year. Some would assume that a 50 percent gain the next year would make the investor whole, but this is not so. The investor would need a **100 percent return** in year two just to be back at the **original investment value.** Even though the average annual return in the example below is 25 percent {(-50 + 100)/2}, the overall return is zero. The investor has gained nothing because of volatility. A modern retirement income plan *MUST* account for volatility.

Sequence of Returns Risk involves the premature erosion of savings due to the actual order in which investment returns occur. If a client is regularly withdrawing money from their portfolio, then some of those withdrawals will be made during a "down" part of the volatility cycle. If these withdrawals occur in the early years of the retiree's retirement, then the likelihood is high that the portfolio will be exhausted before the end of a thirty-year retirement. A modern retirement income plan *MUST* account for sequence risks.

How Bad Timing Can Significantly Erode Savings

Age	Balance	S&P Return	Balance	Yearly Withdrawal	Balance
62	$100,000	11.4%	$111,390	$5,000	$106,390
63	$106,390	29.6%	$137,881	$5,000	$132,881
64	$132,881	13.4%	$150,701	$5,000	$145,701
65	$145,701	0.0%	$145,701	$5,000	$140,701
66	$140,701	12.8%	$158,682	$5,000	$153,682
67	$153,682	23.5%	$189,721	$5,000	$184,721
68	$184,721	-38.5%	$113,622	$5,000	$108,622
69	$108,622	3.5%	$112,456	$5,000	$107,456
70	$107,456	13.6%	$122,092	$5,000	$117,092
71	$117,092	3.0%	$120,604	$5,000	$115,604
72	$115,604	9.0%	$125,997	$5,000	$120,997
73	$120,997	26.4%	$152,916	$5,000	$147,916
74	$147,916	-23.4%	$113,348	$5,000	$108,348
75	$108,348	-13.0%	$94,220	$5,000	$89,220
76	$89,220	-10.1%	$80,173	$5,000	$75,173

The two diagrams show the impact that returns have once you begin taking **regular withdrawals** from your savings. They both begin with $100,000 in savings and show the client withdrawing $5,000 each year. In the first example, returns are positive in the early years: 11.4 percent, 29.6 percent, then 13.4 percent. Negative returns are not experienced until the later years. As a result, the client does not experience severe erosion.

However, in the second example, we invert the returns, so the early years show three consecutive years of *negative* returns with the positive returns occurring later. Notice the impact that these early negative returns, combined with a systematic withdraw of $5,000, has on the portfolio.

Now, instead of having $75,173 in year fifteen, they only have $16,598—raising significant concerns about running out of savings.

Age	Balance	S&P Return	Balance	Yearly Withdrawal	Balance
62	$100,000	-10.1%	$89,860	$$5,000	$84,860
63	$84,860	-13.0%	$73,794	$5,000	$68,794
64	$68,794	-23.4%	$52,717	$5,000	$47,717
65	$47,717	26.4%	$60,305	$5,000	$55,305
66	$55,305	9.0%	$60,277	$5,000	$55,277
67	$55,277	3.0%	$56,935	$5,000	$51,935
68	$51,935	13.6%	$59,009	$5,000	$54,009
69	$54,009	3.5%	$55,915	$5,000	$50,915
70	$50,915	-38.5%	$31,318	$5,000	$26,318
71	$26,318	23.5%	$32,489	$5,000	$27,489
72	$27,489	12.8%	$31,003	$5,000	$26,003
73	$26,003	0.0%	$26,003	$5,000	$21,003
74	$21,003	13.4%	$23,819	$5,000	$18,819
75	$18,819	29.6%	$24,389	$5,000	$19,389
76	$19,389	11.4%	$21,598	$5,000	$16,598

Early volatility, combined with systematic withdrawal, causes significant erosion.

QUESTION: How do we solve the early exhaustion of the portfolio problem?

Case Study: Mitigating Risks and Increasing Longevity With The HECM

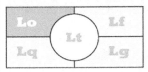 **Client Overview**: Twin brothers, James and John, did everything together. They chose the same jobs, savings rates, and asset allocations; they both retired on the same day from the same company and decided on the same amount they would need from their savings each year. They differed in only one way. Three years ago, they left their shared, long-time advisor and each got a new advisor. They told their respective advisors they felt they could easily achieve a thirty-year retirement, but their shared, nagging concern was whether they had done enough to ensure their savings would last as long as they did.

Planning Objective: Structure their investment accounts to give them the greatest possibility of inflation minded growth with the lowest amount of risk.

The Erosion Solution: Incorporating Housing Wealth

James' advisor had a very active management approach to help mitigate these risks—one which involved changing allocation, reducing the amount of money James takes out during down markets, and other strategies to minimize portfolio erosion and ensure longevity. His advisor's firm stance was that **reverse mortgages should only be used a last resort**—only if James had completely exhausted his existing savings.

John's advisor had a different approach with regards to inflation, volatility, and sequence risk—one that involved housing wealth. He had read the recent research suggesting clients could diminish risk by not withdrawing from the portfolio when the market is down; instead, it was recommended that housing equity be used as a substitute.

Here's how it worked:

- John's advisor suggested he establish a reverse mortgage line of credit (ReLOC) as equity insurance at the onset of his retirement.

- After a $500 out-of-pocket deductible, John had converted his $200,000 home equity into an $80,000 line of credit, growing at around 5 percent.

$200,000	
Year	ReLOC Value
0	$79,396
5	$103,118
10	$133,929
15	$173,945
20	$225,917
25	$309,167
30	$381,086

- His advisor then recommended that if his portfolio experienced a negative return during any given year, John take money the following year not out of his savings, but from the HECM. The ReLOC would function as a non-correlated, buffer asset —providing that year's income, so John's portfolio would have time to recover.

Age	Balance	S&P Return	Balance	Yearly Withdrawal Balance	End of Year
62	$100,000	-10.1%	$89,860	$5,000	$84,860
63	$84,860	-13.0%	$73,794	$0	$73,794
64	$73,794	-23.4%	$56,549	$0	$56,549
65	$56,549	26.4%	$71,466	$0	$71,466
66	$71,466	9.0%	$77,891	$5,000	$72,891
67	$72,891	3.0%	$75,078	$5,000	$70,078
68	$70,078	13.6%	$79,622	$5,000	$74,622
69	$74,622	3.5%	$77,256	$5,000	$72,256
70	$72,256	-38.5%	$44,445	$5,000	$39,445
71	$39,445	23.5%	$48,695	$0	$48,695
72	$48,695	12.8%	$54,918	$5,000	$49,918
73	$49,918	0.0%	$49,918	$5,000	$44,918
74	$44,918	13.4%	$50,941	$5,000	$45,941
75	$45,941	29.6%	$59,540	$5,000	$54,540
76	$54,540	11.4%	$60,752	$5,000	$55,752

Since the reverse mortgage dollars would come out tax-free, John wouldn't need the whole $5,000 per year—resulting in even more money in his savings.

In the diagram, you can see that by not drawing from the securities portfolio following a down year, but drawing from the ReLOC instead, John had nearly $56,000 in year fifteen versus his brother's $16,598. (Imagine if the portfolio had a starting value of $1 million vs. $100K . . .)

Interesting to note: the research done by Dr. Pfau, Dr. Barry Sacks, and Texas Tech showed that the starting account value ($1 million vs. $200,000) mattered very little when using the reverse mortgage line of credit in this way. The basic premise remains the same: if you are make systematic withdrawals from the savings portfolio, *don't convert portfolio assets into dollars during down markets, but rather convert assets from a different source.*

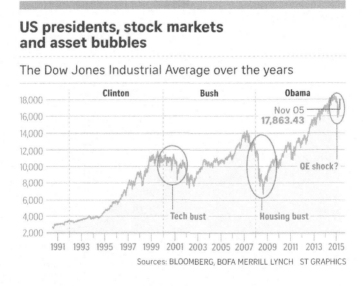

US presidents, stock markets and asset bubbles

The Dow Jones Industrial Average over the years

Sources: BLOOMBERG, BOFA MERRILL LYNCH   ST GRAPHICS

Did the incorporation of housing wealth help meet the planning objective? Remember the objective was to structure his client's portfolio so that the investment account would have the greatest possibility of growth with the lowest amount of long-term risk.

What were the benefits of this strategy?

- *John's portfolio had a significantly greater probability of savings success* than if he had not implemented the strategy (success being defined by how long his savings lasted).

- *John's overall estate value was greater than his brother's.* This means the amount of actual dollars left in the estate was significantly greater.

- *John had a more enjoyable retirement.* By having a back-up plan for risk, volatility, inflation, and sequence risk, John could have greater peace of mind because of the simple insurance strategy his advisor told him about.

Advisor Insights: Mike McGlothlin

Executive Vice President of Ash Brokerage

Advisors across the country are discovering the value in the HECM's ability to increase the longevity of client savings. Here's a comment from the VP of Ash Brokerage:

"Several things surprised me when I first began to learn about HECMs. First of all is their flexibility and how you can use the line of credit. I also like recommending HECMs as a source for non-correlated assets. When we've done some testing with past returns and we've used a HECM to secure income in years following the down market and allowing the portfolios to rebound, we found that we reduced the failure rate in over 2,000 simulations from 26 percent failure at age 95 down to a 2 percent failure rate at age ninety-five. That's a significant change in the probability of success from many Americans that have a significant amount of wealth tied to their homes."

In a sense, longevity is the foundational goal in retirement income planning. It is certainly the main criteria for how success is measured. Other concerns matter far less if a retiree's income doesn't last their whole retirement.

11

Paychecks and Playchecks Re-imagined

Over the years, I've become friends with two retirement income giants, Tom Hegna and Curtis Cloke. Both have popularized the creation of optimized retirement income plans using fixed income vehicles such as indexed, immediate, and deferred income annuities.

Tom coined the phrase **"Paychecks and Playchecks,"** and Curtis used the phrase "**Buy Income and Invest the Difference.**" Both men focus on converting a portion of the portfolio savings (Buy Income) into fixed income (Paychecks) to cover retirement essentials. Then they repurpose the remaining savings (Invest the Difference) in a more aggressive allocation to cover discretionary items (Playchecks).

Again, I must emphasize that the inclusion of these strategies are not meant to provide a blanket endorsement of their efficacy but rather to display how the HECM seamlessly integrates into some of today's most popular planning concepts.

TWO QUESTIONS:

1. Can a reverse mortgage longevity strategy work with clients who are more risk-averse?

2. Can a reverse mortgage give the advisor greater planning flexibility when incorporated with the Paychecks and Playchecks strategy?

CASE STUDY: Creating Longevity for Risk-Averse Clients

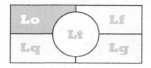 **Client Overview**: Paula (age sixty-five) is the older sister of James and John. She never married, has $1 million invested, and lives in a $375,000 home with no mortgage. She enjoys good restaurants, theater, and travel and is the picture of good health. Not a risk-taker, she is very reluctant to have all her savings in investments that could lose principal. But she also understands the need for dollars in places that can keep pace with inflation.

Planning Objective: Create more fixed income, while leaving more in vehicles that have higher return potential.

Power Question: "Paula, if we could convert some of your assets to:

- Create fixed income to cover your living essentials,

- Allocate assets for lifestyle dollars for enjoyment purposes, and

- Convert another asset to create an inflation buffer that could also be turned into an income stream as needed,

Would you want me to show you how?"

CONVERSATION GUIDE

Step 1

Conversation: Ask Paula to calculate *the amount of money she needs this year to cover her essentials*. Paula tells you $40,000. According to Hegna and Cloke, Paula could convert a *portion* of her investable assets ($1 million) and turn this into guaranteed fixed income for life.

You share this with her, and she's comfortable with the amount she must convert but asks how much more she would need to convert if she wants her monthly income to go up each year to *adjust for inflation*.

The new figure you give her for a 4 percent inflation rider requires a significantly higher lump sum than she feels comfortable with, *so she chooses a 1 percent rider* instead. She reasons that in those years where inflation is more, she will simply live on less.

Step 2

Reallocation: Since you have now covered Paula's income essentials (Paychecks), you can re-allocate her remaining securities assets into vehicles that have greater growth potential to combat inflation (Playchecks).

Question: Is there anything more you can do to optimize Paula's retirement?

Answer: *Yes, you can covert her $375,000 home into a $147,900 line of credit that is currently growing at 4.5 percent.*

Step 3

Imagination: The client now has several options by which to use her HECM line of credit (see diagram).

The chart below illustrates how Paula's plan has just improved. Notice the three sources of income: (A) the fixed monthly income from the annuities. This will adjust 1% each year. (B) The investments that remain, which can now be positioned to grow more aggressively. (C) The $147,900 HECM line of credit, which can grow or be converted to monthly income at any point during the loan.

(A) FIXED INCOME	(B) INVESTMENTS		(C) HECM LINE OF CREDIT	
Essentials	Enjoyment		Inflation Protection	Income Protection
$40,000 1% Adjustment	($200 – $400k) 4%, 8%, 12%	YEAR	ReLOC Growth	Monthly Payment
$40,000		0	$147,900	$791
$42,040		5	$189,680	$1,083
$44,184		10	$243,428	$1,556
$46,438		15	$312,405	$2,357
$48,807		20	$400,928	$3,989
$51,297		25	$514,535	$8,252

Flexibility and Peace of Mind: Five New Housing Wealth Possibilities

1. Instead of converting the portfolio to create $40,000 of income, you can convert *less* and use the HECM monthly payment of $791 in its place ($9,492 a year). Paula can then convert enough to cover $30,000 of needed income, combining this with the HECM monthly payment and leaving a larger Playcheck to grow for her.

2. Paula can choose a larger inflation rider on her $40,000—requiring a larger lump sum and *less* in her Playchecks bucket—but then use the guaranteed growth of the ReLOC to serve as *another Playchecks bucket.*

3. Paula can use the ReLOC as a growth bucket and take additional dollars in the years that it's needed. In this way, the HECM functions as its own *inflation rider.*

4. Paula can use the growing ReLOC. Down the road as her needs change, she can turn on the monthly payment feature, which would be considerably larger at that time, and use it to supplement her needs. It now serves as a type of income rider.

5. Paula can also make use of the ReLOC bi-directionality feature and repay any funds drawn from the line of credit or *stop* the monthly payments once they've started. She could do this from portfolio gains, un-needed required minimum distributions, tax returns, etc. Every dollar she repays to the HECM line of credit goes into the line and continues to grow, and Paula can take this out at any time in the future.

As you can see, the ReLOC serves as a type of inflation protection/rider, allowing Paula to draw money in the years or months she may need something extra and then pay it back if she wants. The ReLOC's ability to be seamlessly converted into a monthly payment now functions as a type of deferred income rider. Paula's essential needs are covered with fixed income, her enjoyment needs are covered with a more aggressive investment allocation, and her inflation protection is covered by the reverse mortgage.

It's hard to argue with the practical wisdom of the Paychecks/ Playchecks and "Buy Income/Invest the Difference" strategies. It's even harder to improve upon them, but by combining guaranteed income, equity-based investments, and housing wealth, you can give your client new options and tremendous peace of mind. (Not to mention that you look like a retirement savant.)

12

Create Guilt-Free Retirement with a HECM 4326 Replacement

> *"Paying off the mortgage after 30 years followed by retirement used to be a rite of passage for many, but this scenario is no longer the norm."*
>
> **– Investopedia.com**

Carrying a mortgage payment in retirement will be the most significant financial challenge most existing retirees and emerging baby boomers will face. Upwards of 68 percent will have some sort of monthly, housing-related debt payment in retirement (mortgages, second mortgages, home equity loans, or lines of credit).

Don't think it's true? The next time you are with a gathering of boomers, just ask how many have some sort of mortgage/home loan payment. It may surprise you!

When you combine a house payment with low savings and longer life expectancy, helping your clients eliminate a monthly mortgage payment and create cash flow could be a real game-changer.

Three Phases of Retirement and the Danger of Overspending

Retirement can generally be separated into three phases. In my podcast interview with Tom Hegna, he described the three phases like this:

"A lot of people think retirement is going to be thirty to forty years of golf, tennis, cruises, and line dancing. I tell people that's not true. You are going to go through three distinct phases. The first phase is what I call the **Go-Go years**. Now, during the Go-Go years, you are playing golf, you are playing tennis, you are going on cruises, you are line dancing, and every day it's happy hour somewhere.

But make no mistake about it: the Go-Go years are going to be followed by the **Slow-Go years**. Now, during the Slow-Go years, you can still do everything you did in the Go-Go years, you just don't want to anymore. In fact, you don't want to go downtown after 4:30 because Dad can't see when it's dark out. That's the Slow-Go years.

And the Slow-Go years are going to be followed by the **No-Go years.** The No-Go years are those years where you are probably not leaving the building until you're leaving the building, if you know what I am talking about."

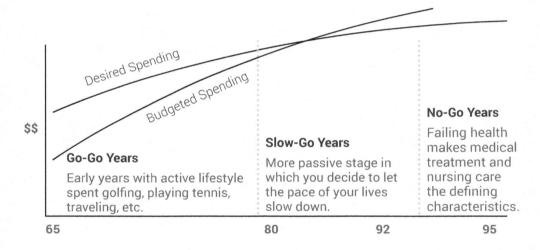

$$ \$\$ $$

Go-Go Years

Early years with active lifestyle spent golfing, playing tennis, traveling, etc.

Slow-Go Years

More passive stage in which you decide to let the pace of your lives slow down.

No-Go Years

Failing health makes medical treatment and nursing care the defining characteristics.

65   80   92   95

It's important to note that your client's income desires are typically greater during the early phases of retirement because that's when they tend to be most active. Look at the illustration and notice the two lines. The top line is the **desired spending,** and the second line is the **budgeted spending.** At the onset of retirement, there is a larger gap between desired spending and budgeted spending. This is what happens when the husband desires to spend $100 a week for golf but his wife reminds him of the budget, or when the wife wants to go on short vacation and her husband reminds her of the budget!

The truth is that most retirees' *spending desires exceed their allowable budget*, and this is most clearly felt in the early phases. This dilemma causes them to make some very serious choices. The majority include rolling the dice, spending more, and hoping that somehow things work out, that their investments perform better than expected, or perhaps that they may not live as long as projected. None of these choices are strategically responsible, though clients choose them regularly.

But what if there was a simple strategy that could help solve this issue?

CASE STUDY: HECM Replacement—The Power of Eliminating a Mortgage Payment

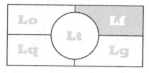

Client Overview: Pierce and Linda have re-tired. They have investments of $300,000, and their existing budget combines draws from their portfolio, Social Security, their pension, and a few annuities to cover their monthly living essentials. They also have an $800 monthly mortgage payment for the next twenty-five years. Their home is valued at $400,000, and their mortgage balance is $150,000.

They are satisfied that their budget will get them to the finish line but are disappointed that it does not allow enough money for the lifestyle they envisioned, including visiting their three children and six grandchildren, who all live out of town.

Planning Objective: Help the clients use current retirement assets to restructure expenses, increase cash flow, and provide additional reserves for discretionary spending.

This objective leads us to ask: **Can eliminating a monthly mortgage payment help their lifestyle?**

The Single Most Powerful Question You Can Ask Your Clients

The most important question to ask your clients is, "What would life be like if you didn't have to make a monthly mortgage payment?"

That's it. This single question can unlock so many planning doors that it's almost unfair to your competitors. The question works not only with your older clients, but with their children. Let's walk through a simple conversation to see how it works.

CONVERSATION GUIDE

Power Question

"Pierce, Linda, may I ask you an honest question? **What would retirement be like if you didn't have to make a monthly mortgage payment?**"

Answer: *"It would be great not to have to make that monthly payment." (Note: Sometimes the clients say their mortgage payment is not an issue. We will address that response in the next chapter.)*

Question 2

"Why would it be great? Can you tell me more about the difference not having a mortgage payment would make in your lives?"

At this point, your clients will begin to share about aspects of their retirement that they may not have shared before. Often, they will tell you that they'd like to have more money to spend (Lifestyle Concern), or they don't want to draw as much from savings as they are (Longevity Concern), or they want to be able to save money for a rainy day (Liquidity/Long-Term Care

Concern), or they would love to send some money to help their grandchildren save for college or private school (Legacy Concern).

"If there were a way we could eliminate your monthly mortgage payment, so you could (list their desires), would you be open to seeing how it works?"

Asking and exploring this *one simple question* helps your clients gain awareness of their financial goals and hone in on their desires and dreams. Having this type of laser-focused dialogue also helps you, the advisor, suggest the appropriate adjustments to help them achieve the retirement they want.

How Does It Work?

In Column A, we see that Pierce and Linda have $300,000 in savings, growing at 4 percent. They need to withdraw $2,000 per month for their current lifestyle. In this simplified example, assuming nothing changes, they will run out of money in seventeen years and two months.

However, as noted in Column B, if the clients use the HECM to eliminate their existing mortgage loan, a few things happen:

- The HECM will make money available to them based on the age of the youngest borrower, value of the home, and current interest rate at the time. In this case, the HECM made $175,000 available, which pays off the $150,000 mortgage balance.

- The client can reduce their $2,000 monthly savings draw by $800 (their old mortgage payment). Their new draw is now **$1,200 per month.**

- The portfolio then lasts a full thirty years. In fact, they will still have $148,000 remaining in year thirty.

Results Summary

	A Traditional Mortgage	B With a HECM Replacement
Starting amount	$300,000	$300,000
Years you wish to make withdrawals	30 years	30 years
Periodic withdrawal from savings	$2,000 per month	$1,200 per month
Rate of return	4% compounded annually	4% compounded annually
Total amount you will have withdrawn	$411,386	$432,386
Ending balance	$0 (at 17 years, 2 months)	$148,002 (at 30 years)

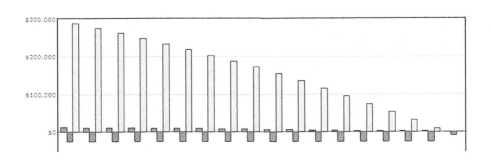

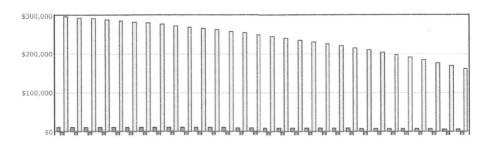

Charts and Graphs are for Illustration Purposes Only: Interest rate shown at 4% annual, no inflation adjustment factored, and marginal tax brackets are not considered.
https://www.calcxml.com/calculators/how-long-will-my-money-last

Did the HECM replacement meet the planning objectives of helping the clients use current retirement assets to restructure expenses, increase cash flow, and provide additional reserves for discretionary spending?

The answer is "mostly," but we still have one simple tweak.

Bridging the Desired Spending Gap

Sometimes your client has enough savings to sustain their spending rate (Longevity), but they don't feel they have enough to cover their discretionary spending (Lifestyle). How can this strategy address that concern? Very easily.

Through the HECM 4326 Replacement, your client was able to eliminate an $800 (or whatever the amount) existing monthly mortgage payment. We now have $800 more per month, or close to $10,000 per year, in additional cash flow that they can use during the Go-Go years.

The HECM exchange bridges the gap between what they *desired* and what is *budgeted* without making them hold their breath for a positive outcome with an uncertain future. The money they need for lifestyle/discretionary spending is provided.

When you consider the large number of retirees who are carrying some sort of loan payment into retirement, you have the basis for many conversations that can be broached with the client themselves and even their children, but only if you are willing to ask.

Power Question: Would having an extra $800 per month make a difference in your retirement enjoyment?

13

The Advisor's Most Neglected Planning Opportunity

I n the last chapter, we talked about the pervasive nature of mortgage debt and the heavy burden it places on those entering retirement. However, the widespread nature of the problem makes it one of the most common planning opportunities for advisors. If you're not talking about mortgage debt with your clients, you are missing something major.

What If There's a Shortfall?

Sometimes the proceeds from a reverse mortgage are *not enough* to pay off the existing mortgage obligations (which is a requirement). Many advisors would dismiss the reverse mortgage at this point, but that could be an opportunity lost.

The chart below shows a reverse mortgage making $175,000 available, but in this example, the clients' existing mortgage debts total $200,000. They have a shortfall of $25,000. When this happens, the clients can choose to move the additional dollars needed from other savings if they have them available, but is this a good idea?

For instance, the client has $300,000 in their investment account as well as money in cash equivalents, a small annuity they aren't drawing from, and $50,000 of cash value in life insurance.

HECM Benefit	$175,000	Investments	$300,000
Total Loan Balances	$200,000	Cash/CD/Money Market	$40,000
Shortfall to Close	$25,000	Existing Annuities	$50,000
Monthly Principal/ Interest Payments	$2,000	Cash Value Life Insurance	$50,000

Should the client take money from other savings to add to the HECM and pay off their existing mortgage? The answer to this question lies mainly in how important it is to the clients' longevity and lifestyle concerns to be free of the monthly mortgage payment.

CONVERSATION GUIDE

Power Question

Is eliminating a monthly mortgage payment to have greater retirement security something that's important for you to accomplish now, or would you be willing to wait?

If wait: Broach the topic again in a few years.
If now: Go to question two.

Question 2

Would you be comfortable pulling $25,000 from some of your savings if it meant greater peace of mind and retirement security?

If no: Go back to question one.
If yes: Go to question three.

Question 3

Which account(s) would it make the most sense to use in paying off the $25,000 shortfall: the high tax or low/no tax?

If high tax: share the financial impact.
If low/no tax: share the financial impact.

What you may discover is that clients who have the resources are more than willing to draw from those savings to rid themselves of the burden of having a monthly loan payment. In this example, would it make sense for the client to draw money out of the cash, CDs, or money market funds? Those funds do not produce much growth, and the tax consequence is very small compared to the benefit.

In some cases, clients will choose to replenish the account from which they withdrew those funds. As a result, they continue to "make a payment," but this time it's back to the funds they used and not to the bank. In either scenario, there is flexibility.

Are You Missing Planning Opportunities?

The other day, an advisor said that he doesn't have regular conversations with what he called his "transactional" clients—those who had purchased an annuity or some sort of insurance policy. I told him he was missing some significant planning opportunities by not engaging them in ongoing dialogue.

How many of those retired, "transactional" clients own a home? In most cases, the answer is 80 to 90 percent. How many of those have some sort of mortgage-related payment? Recent studies tell us that up to 68 percent of them will.

If you asked those clients what retirement would be like if they didn't ever have to make a mandatory mortgage payment again, what percentage of those clients would express some sense of relief? Those are the clients with whom you want to make contact.

Here's an example of an advisor who has had 1,000 "transactional" clients, or perhaps an advisor who has wealth management clients, but feels they no longer have anything to invest or any planning opportunities that warrant the advisor's attention.

Power of Missed Opportunity	
Total Transactional Clients	1,000
Over Age 62	800
62+ and Own a Home	700
Still Have a Loan Payment	500

Out of those 1,000 clients, how many are over the age of sixty-two (80%), own a home (87%), and have some sort of mortgage payment?

Based on those figures, somewhere between 400 to 500 of his existing "transactional" clients might have a need for the increased cash flow and financial flexibility that an integrated housing wealth strategy could provide.

What else could that client do with the $500, $1,000, or $1,500 monthly payment many of them are carrying into retirement? How could that extra cash flow enhance their longevity, liquidity, lifestyle, etc.? You won't know if you never ask.

Thank Heaven for 7-11: Expanding Your Planning Possibilities

Advisors are not always in front of retirees, but they may be in front of their children, or even grandchildren. Herein lies a tremendous, hidden opportunity that most advisors will never uncover. But you can with these seven magic words:

Do your parents currently own their home?

That's the power question, because 87 percent of their parents do own their home!

Your clients will most likely say, "Yes, they do. Why do you ask?"

In response, you would ask the second power question:

Are your parents 100 percent certain they'll have a great retirement?

This question will generate tons of conversation because Mom and Dad are always sharing with their children something about their finances. It happens at holiday dinners, summer vacations, and even in routine conversations. It comes out when parents say things like, "I wish I could have done more for Christmas, but we just didn't have the money this year." Or, "We'd love to visit more, but right now we have to be mindful of the budget." "Somedays I wish I'd never refinanced this home; I had no idea what a burden this monthly payment would be once I retired."

Children hear these types of comments all the time—more than they realize. Often, it's not until an advisor asks them a pointed question that their parents' comments are recalled.

When you ask, be sure to have a notepad to write down the concerns and comments.

Lastly, ask: "If there were a way we could help them {mention goals from your notepad}, would they be open to hearing more?"

I think by this point in the book, you'll know where to go from here, but you can't get there unless you engage the children. Thank heaven for 7-11! If you hadn't noticed, the questions have seven words and eleven words, respectively.

Acres of Diamonds

Advisors are missing planning opportunities they didn't even know existed; in the midst of everyday life as an advisor, that's not hard to do. Our tendency, then, is to begin looking elsewhere to find new clients and new planning opportunities when the real treasure may be closer than we think.

In the late 1800s, Russell Conwell, the founder of Temple University, heard a parable while traveling through present-day Iraq.

There was once a wealthy man who lived not far from the river. He was contented because he was wealthy, and wealthy because he was contented. One day, a priest visited him and told him about diamonds. The wealthy man listened and heard all about diamonds, how much they were worth and all they could do and went to his bed that night a poor man. He had not lost anything, but he was poor because he was discontented, and discontented because he feared he was poor.

He sold his farm, left his family, and traveled to faraway places searching for diamonds. He did not find them. His health and his wealth failed him. Dejected, he cast himself into the sea.

One day, the man who had purchased the wealthy man's farm found a curious sparkling stone in a stream that cut through his land. It was a diamond. Digging produced more diamonds—acres of diamonds, in fact. This, according to the parable, was the discovery of the famed diamonds of Golconda.

The moral of the story is plain: many people (advisors and/or their clients) feel discontented and go searching for exotic solutions when the real answers are much closer than they realize—well within their reach . . . perhaps even in their own homes.

With that in mind, I have a challenge for you: look at your current clients, along with the new ones you are acquiring, and ask one simple question, "How could your life be different if you didn't have to make a monthly loan payment?" Or contact their adult sons and daughters to ask, "How would your parents' lives be different if they didn't have to make a monthly loan payment?"

Acres of diamonds, right there.

14

Turn a HECM Payment into a Million Dollar Safety Net

In this chapter, I will share a HECM housing wealth strategy that is revolutionizing how advisors optimize retirement income plans for the big-ticket items in retirement. It's a strategy that has been around for 30 years but has not been widely presented. As a matter of fact, the software used to model these types of outcomes was just rolled out in 2017!

In the myriad of sobering retirement statistics, there is one that stands out more than most. It seems to be frequently overlooked and neglected in planning conversations: health care. Recent studies show that the typical retiring couple can expect to spend at least $275,000 in out-of-pocket costs on health care; that does not include the additional $130,000 needed for long-term care.

Who Needs Long-Term Care?

- Annually, 8,357,100 people receive support from the five main, long-term care services: home health agencies (4,742,500), nursing homes (1,383,700), hospices (1,244,500), residential care communities (713,300), and adult day service centers (273,200).

- An estimated twelve million Americans needed long-term care in 2007.

- Most people in need of long-term care are elderly.

- The lifetime probability of becoming disabled in at least two activities of daily living, or of being cognitively impaired, is 68% for people age sixty-five and older.

You can find more statistics in the appendix, or at
www.longtermcare.gov or
https://www.caregiver.org/selected-long-term-care-statistics.

If You Like Your Payment, You Can Keep Your Payment

What can an advisor do to help prepare their clients? Many pro-active advisors are already working hard to plan for the realities of health care and long-term care, but I want to show you one simple strategy that when combined with the others you may be using, could make a huge impact.

In the last chapter, I spoke about the HECM replacement strategy for those who don't want the burden of making a payment. Keeping that strategy in mind as we talk about how it could be helpful for clients who **don't mind making a monthly payment**. I think you will be amazed at what can be accomplished.

CASE STUDY: The Hecm Exchange—The Power of Keeping a Mortgage Payment

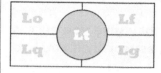

Client Overview: David and Karen are preparing to retire. Both are in good health and believe they will live a long time. They eat right, exercise, and have saved modestly well for retirement. They have four children and seven grandchildren. They currently own a $400,000 home with a $100,000 mortgage balance on which they are paying $1,000 per month for the next thirteen years. Karen's main concern is long-term and health care costs, while David is preoccupied with the lifestyle concern.

CONVERSATION GUIDE

Power Question

David and Karen, what would retirement be like if you didn't have to make a monthly mortgage payment?

A: It would be about the same. The payments aren't a burden to us; we're pretty comfortable.

Question 2

Great, let me make sure I understand. You have been paying your mortgage company $1,000 per month for at least the last seventeen years, correct? In that time, you've paid them over $200,000, and you're financially comfortable continuing those payments?

A: Yes.

Question 3

If you were to call them right now and ask them to send you a check for $80,000 because you had a need, would they send it? Absolutely not, right? They would say you have to apply for a new loan, have your credit run, produce new income documents, get approved, etc. **Why wouldn't they give you access to the money you've paid over the years, especially if you had a pressing need?**

A: I don't know. That's just the way the system works!

Q: How likely is it that you will need access to additional retirement dollars in the future?

A: I would say fairly likely, especially if we live long enough.

Q: What type of things will retirees such as yourself need money for in the future?

A: Increasing taxes, health care, home repairs, unexpected expenses, loss of savings, helping children, you name it.

Final Question

If there was a way you could take the mortgage payments you are already making and create up to an $850,000 reserve for health care and other concerns you mentioned, would you want me to tell you about it?

A: Absolutely, but what do you mean?

Conversation Starter

"Since you are comfortable making payments, *I don't want you to stop.* I want you to continue making the same $1,000 payment on the same day and for the same period of time your current mortgage payments would have lasted. The only change I want you to make is WHO you make the payment to."

How Clients Can Pay Themselves, Not Banks

It's a simple strategy. David and Karen *keep their payment* but change their payment partner. That's it.

What will this do for them? Very simply:

- For every dollar they pay towards the loan, the outstanding balance is reduced (just like it is today), and

- They have access to nearly $300,000 in ten years, or nearly $900,000 in thirty!

You read it correctly! This strategy takes the monthly mortgage payments David and Karen would have been paying anyway and uses them to reduce the outstanding balance of the HECM, while simultaneously adding funds to the available and growing line of credit for tax-free access in the future.

How does the HECM 4326 Exchange work? We simply exchange their existing mortgage for a HECM reverse mortgage. This eliminates the *requirement* of making monthly loan payments.

After that, we suggest that the client *continue making the same payment* they had been making for the last seventeen years. By doing this, they turn on a little-known feature of the HECM. For every dollar paid, the outstanding principal is reduced, *and* the line of credit is increased.

Recall from an earlier chapter how the HECM line of credit works: the $200,000 **principal limit** is determined by the client's age, the value of their home and current interest rate. The **outstanding balance** covers the existing loan they had, which is paid off and used to financed closing costs. The difference between the two is the **available line of credit**.

GROWTH OF THE HECM LINE OF CREDIT

	Year 0	Year 1
Principal Limit	$200,000	$210,000
Outstanding Balance	$115,000	$120,250
Available Line of Credit	$85,000	$89,250

The HECM line of credit has a built-in, guaranteed growth factor, so it grows each year by the underlying note rate. For this example, we are using 5 percent. At the end of year one, the principal limit and the outstanding loan balance both grew, therefore the line of credit has grown from **$85,000 to $89,500 (see table).**

However, as David and Karen continue making their monthly payment, notice what happens.

A total payment of $12,000 was made during the initial year, so the outstanding balance goes DOWN and, consequently, the line of credit balance goes UP even faster than it would have had no payment been made at all! Instead of being $89,500, it's $101,250.

	Year 0	Year 1 without Payment	Year 1 with Payment
Principal Limit	$200,000	$210,000	$210,000
Outstanding Balance	$115,000	$120,250	$108,750
Available Line of Credit	$85,000	$89,250	$101.250

As they continue to make payments, the loan balance continues to decline, but the line of credit balance exponentially increases. By year fourteen, they are no longer making a monthly payment, yet the *accessible line of credit continues to grow!*

	Year 1	Year 2	Year 7
Principal Limit	$210,000	$220,500	$281,420
Outstanding Balance	$108,750	$102,188	$64,112
Available Line of Credit	$101,250	$118,312	$217,308

Did you see it? Let's look at it another way:

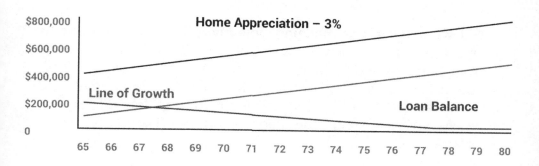

In the chart, the top line reflects the home's appreciating value. The descending line shows the decrease in the outstanding loan balance because of the client making a payment, and the middle line shows the corresponding increasing line of credit.

By the time the clients reach year thirteen, their loan balance is $125, and the available line of credit is well over $300,000.

No Behavioral Change Required

You may now by wondering: what does having this reserve do for your client, what is its value, what problems can it solve, and what peace of mind can it bring?

Giving your clients access to a giant reserve of home equity not only addresses the long-term/health care concerns but encompasses a myriad of other planning opportunities along the way.

Here's the most important element of this strategy: Implementing doesn't require a new behavior pattern, just a new payment partner. Otherwise, their current economic behavior doesn't change one bit. Advisors don't have to convince their clients to change what they're already doing! After all, isn't asking your client to make a financial behavior change the hardest part of planning?

Their payment comes out of the same bank account for the same amount on the same day each month! And the payments remain voluntary and flexible, so they can choose the payment that works best for them at the time. One month, they could pay either $1,000 or $500, and the next month pay either $1,500 or nothing at all. It's 100 percent flexible.

Did we achieve our planning objective? The objective was to create a plan that helps David and Karen prepare for the out-of-pocket costs of health and long-term care—ensuring that adequate reserves are in place, risks are insured, and assets are protected. Additionally, help develop a strategy for using assets wisely while enjoying retirement. To answer the question, let's consider that:

- In fifteen years, David and Karen will have access to more than $415,000 in their HECM line of credit and no more monthly loan payments.

- Karen no longer needs to worry about paying for long-term care should they need it; she now has a back-up plan.

- During the spring and fall, if they wanted, the client could decrease their monthly payment amount (so David has a little extra money for golf). During the winter, they can take their required minimum distributions or tax returns to pay down the HECM and add to the line of credit if they wanted. The point is that they have flexibility.

- They also have peace of mind should any other spending shock surprise them.

I'd say this strategy not only meets but exceeds the planning objectives.

With that in mind, I have one last question:

Why would any retiree have a traditional monthly mortgage payment if they could use the HECM Exchange strategy?

Power Question: If we could take your monthly mortgage payments and turn them into a line of credit that would be available for health and long-term care protection when you needed it, would that be worth investigating?

15

The Sleeping Giant of Reverse Mortgages:

Finding New Retirement Savings

❝ Would it be okay if we increased your cash flow, decreased your expenses, and added more money back into your retirement savings?"

Wow, what a question to ask a client!

In this chapter, I will share a type of reverse mortgage that has become the fastest-growing usage of the tool and the number one technique advisors are using to create **liquidity** and add **new investable dollars** back into their client's retirement.

Those two things are undoubtedly very important. Having access to money when it's needed most is an essential concern when designing retirement income plans, but finding and creating such access is not always as simple. Adding new dollars back into savings in light of current savings rates and longevity concerns is critical. Let me share how to proverbially kill two birds with one housing wealth stone.

Three Types of Liquidity

Before we explore the strategy, let's take a moment to consider the three basic types of liquidity.

1. **Technical Liquidity**: The client has $1,000,000 in retirement savings, but their budget only allows them to safely draw 4 percent per year ($40,000) to adjust for inflation each year. For them to maintain the "safe" budget, they cannot touch the $1,000,000. It's held hostage. Even though they have a large amount of funds (liquidity), they cannot really utilize it without the possibility of jeopardizing its longevity.

2. **Emotional Liquidity**: The client has money in cash, CDs, money markets, or their equivalent and though they realize the money isn't working to its highest potential, they hang onto it because it meets their emotional need to have an easily accessible rainy-day reserve. Though they have access to reserves, they don't have the emotional freedom to use them or reallocate them to vehicles that could generate a much better return.

3. **True Liquidity**: The client has emotionally free, tax-advantaged access to retirement dollars when needed. They have a reserve established for emergencies, expenses, or enjoyment needs that arise. It's always there for them, and they don't feel bad using it.

With that in mind, how can housing wealth be used to achieve true liquidity for your clients?

One way we have already discussed is to implement standard ReLOC or do a HECM replacement and establish a line of credit. This creates cash flow as well as some cushion. However, another strategy is to help them reimagine their retirement income story altogether.

CASE STUDY: Using the HECM for Purchase to Add $226,000 to Clients' Savings

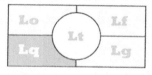

Client Overview: Mark and Linda have just retired and are in good health. They have $405,000 in their portfolio and need to draw $32,000 the first year to maintain their lifestyle. They have a 4,000-square foot home valued at $550,000, on which they still owe $100,000 (with a $1,400 monthly payment).

One has a traditional long-term care policy, and the other has a life policy with a long-term care rider.

Linda's primary concern is **running out of savings**. She has done some online calculating and believes they don't have enough to sustain their $32,000/year draw and adjust for inflation.

Mark had planned to play more golf, maintain his club membership, and travel during the early years of retirement, but Linda's worry about budget is taking the fun out of his golden years.

Planning Objective: Help Mark and Linda use their current assets to dramatically increase retirement savings, while at the same time creating additional monthly cash flow to enjoy their retirement more today.

CONVERSATION GUIDE

Power Question

"Would it be okay if we increased your cash flow, decreased your expenses, and added more money back into your retirement savings?"

How might Mark and Linda answer that question? With a resounding YES, of course. You would then move on to the second question.

Question 2

"Would you be comfortable moving to a different home if it meant we could create additional income, you wouldn't have to worry about running out of money, and Mark could play more golf?

The Sleeping Giant

In 2008, as part of the Housing and Economic Recovery Act (HERA), the U.S. Department of Housing authorized an entirely new type of home equity conversion mortgage—the **HECM for**

Purchase (H4P). This loan allows retirees to purchase a new home with the proceeds of the HECM on the new home financing a portion of the purchase price. A new home can be purchased for about 50 to 60 percent down with no monthly mortgage payments. The process can even begin prior to moving in.

This addition to the HECM program opened an entirely new world of planning opportunities for advisors—its superpower being the ability to create true liquidity.

Here's how it works, using Mark and Linda's example (see illustration):

Step A: Mark and Linda sell their existing home, pay the realtor costs and transfer taxes, and have $500,000 left over.

Step B: They pay off their outstanding mortgage of $100,000. This frees them from the tyranny of the mandatory monthly mortgage payment.

Step C: They now have $400,000 left to put towards their next home. They can choose to move to a more expensive $500,000 home (upsize), to a similarly priced $400,000 home (same-size), or to a less expensive $300,000 home (downsize).

Step D: Mark and Linda choose to move to a $300,000 home. They have a few financing options:

1. **They can use the $400,000 from the sale of their old house to pay cash for the new home and have $100,000 left.**

   Potential concern: Now that they've locked most of their money in the property, what happens if another housing correction happens? What happens if they cannot get the money out of the property when they need it? *Keeping proceeds liquid versus locked is advantageous during times of uncertainty.*

2. **They can make a smaller down payment in cash and take out a traditional loan.**

Potential concern: They are now back at square one with mandatory monthly mortgage payments.

3. **They can draw money from retirement savings and pay for all or a portion of the new home that way.**

. Potential concern: This unnecessarily cannibalizes their savings and sacrifices the growth they might need for future years.

4. **They can use the HECM for Purchase (H4P) to finance a portion of the home's purchase.** The H4P will finance around 40 to 50 percent based on their ages and current interest rates.

Step E: They choose option #4, the HECM for Purchase. The amount of proceeds available to them is based on the age of the youngest borrower, the value of the home they're buying, and the current interest rates. In this illustration, the H4P makes $126,000 available to them.

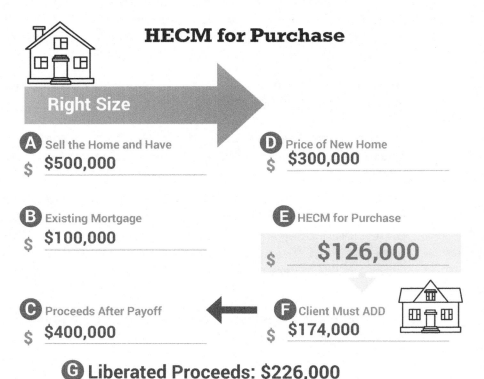

HECM for Purchase

Right Size

Ⓐ Sell the Home and Have
$ **$500,000**

Ⓓ Price of New Home
$ **$300,000**

Ⓑ Existing Mortgage
$ **$100,000**

Ⓔ HECM for Purchase
$ **$126,000**

Ⓒ Proceeds After Payoff
$ **$400,000**

Ⓕ Client Must ADD
$ **$174,000**

Ⓖ Liberated Proceeds: $226,000

Step F: They must add $174,000 of their own funds (sale price of home - H4P proceeds = $174,000).

Step G: After using $174,000 from their proceeds, they now have $226,000 left over.

Did you see it? That one statement is so powerful, it bears re-peating: *the clients now have $226,000 in liberated proceeds from the sale of their home.*

The benefits are obvious:

+ A new home

+ No monthly mortgage payments

+ No money taken from savings

+ Preservation of some sale proceeds

+ $226,000 in additional funds

Did we accomplish the planning goals for the client? Recall that our goal was to help Mark and Linda use their current assets to dramatically increase retirement savings while at the same time creating additional monthly cash flow to enjoy their retirement more today.

Did we increase cash flow? Yes. By eliminating the monthly mortgage payment, we created $1,400 more in monthly cash flow—more than enough for Mark to enjoy golf without guilt!

Did we reduce expenses? Yes. By moving them from a $550,000 home (which needed some maintenance) to a newer $300,000 home with lower taxes, newer appliances, and lower maintenance costs, we have lowered their monthly expenditures.

Did we add new dollars into retirement savings? Absolutely! Mark and Linda were able to add $226,000 dollars to their savings. With the help of their trusted advisor, they can now re-purpose those dollars to create even greater retirement efficiencies. Additionally, we created true liquidity and met their legacy goals.

Can Clients Buy Their More Expensive Dream Home?

You can use the H4P to upsize, downsize, or same-size; the principles are the same. The H4P allows the clients to purchase their next home with around 50 to 60 percent down and have no monthly mortgage payments.

Consider another example: Sam was a retired advisor who sold his practice to his daughter. He decided to sell his home and received $400,000 in proceeds. He wanted to buy a home that cost $500,000. Actually, that was the base model; he and his wife really wanted the $600,000 model. They had a few options:

They could move to a $400,000 same-size home and use all the proceeds from their sale.

They could get the $500,000 house they had originally wanted, use the sale proceeds, and then either take out a $100,000 mortgage or use $100,000 from their savings.

They could get the $600,000 house they really wanted, use all the sale proceeds, and either take out a $200,000 mortgage or move that amount from savings.

They could use the HECM for Purchase (see below) which would make $267,000 available for the house they really wanted. They would have to use $333,000 from their sale proceeds, leaving them with $67,000. They wouldn't have to take out a mortgage and make payments, and they wouldn't have to use money from savings.

Proceeds from Sale	New Home Price	HECM Proceeds	Down Payment	Liberated Proceeds
$400,000	$600,000	$267,000	$333,000	$67,000
$400,000	$500,000	$210,000	$290,000	$110,000
$400,000	$400,000	$168,000	$232,000	$168,000

Which option do you think they chose? If you said the last one, utilizing H4P, you would be correct. You can see from the example above that the H4P gave Sam and his wife flexibility. They can move into the more expensive home and still have liberated dollars remaining!

Out-of-the-Box Thinking Shows You Have the Clients' Best Interest in Mind

Very rarely does something come along that can reimagine a client's whole retirement picture, but the HECM for Purchase allows for this.

There are millions of emerging baby boomers and existing retirees whose lives will be long and whose savings may not be adequate. How many would be receptive to being asked:

"If there was a way we could increase your cash flow, decrease your expenses, and add more money back into your retirement savings, would you want to discuss it?"

Or, **"Would you be comfortable having a conversation about moving to a different home if it meant we could create additional income and add significantly more new dollars into your savings?"**

Whether your clients choose this option or not, they will be glad to know that you are thinking outside the box and have their best interest in mind, especially when compared to the myriad of advisors who have no idea how to use this strategy.

A recent study revealed that more than 50 percent of retirees are open to moving, but many just don't know how it would be possible. Some wonder where they could go after selling their home and paying off the mortgage. Using a simple diagram like the one below can show them how they can take their home sale proceeds to buy their next home with as little as 50 to 60 percent down and eliminate their monthly mortgage payments. This conversation is a real game-changer.

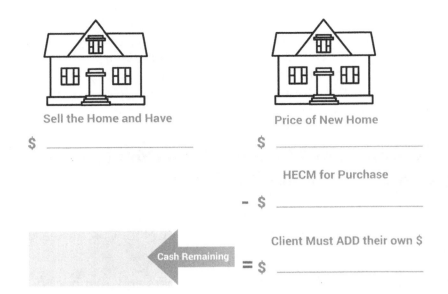

Sell the Home and Have

$ _____

Price of New Home

$ _____

HECM for Purchase

- $ _____

Client Must ADD their own $

Cash Remaining

= $ _____

The Reality of Our Jobs as Advisors

Last week, I spoke with an estate planning attorney whose clients (age seventy-two and seventy-seven) were living in a $1.1 million home. They loved their six-bedroom, four-bath, three-story, 4,000 square foot mini-mansion. The problem was that they were carrying $180,000 in mortgage debt, had exhausted most of their savings, and had run up significant credit card debt. Living on Social Security and two very small pensions, they had a severe cash flow problem.

They were given two housing wealth options:

1) Pursue a traditional HECM replacement. It would pay off the mortgage, eliminate the credit card debt, and leave about $200,000 left over.

2) Sell the home; use the proceeds to pay off the mortgage, credit cards, realtor costs, and transfer taxes; and have around $800,000 left over. Using the HECM for purchase program, they could then buy a $500,000 home for around $250,000 down. This means they would have $550,000 left to add to their retirement savings. They'd have no monthly mortgage payments and minimal to no upkeep/maintenance.

At the time of this writing, they are still deciding. They serve as a good reminder that it's not up to the advisor to push one way or another; our job is simply to ensure that housing wealth is part of the retirement income conversation.

16

Converting Assets for a Tax-Free Retirement:

The Roth IRA Conversation

Recall the Mount Everest illustration from an earlier chapter. On the way up the mountain, the accumulation period, advisors are concerned about helping their clients acquire money and ensure their assets are properly allocated to maximize growth while minimizing risk.

However, as retirement commences, and clients begin the descent down the mountain, a different focus emerges—drawing income from those funds. But where should they draw money from first?

Traditionally, retirees have had three retirement income sources from which to choose:

- **Taxable**: CDs, Brokerage Accounts, etc.

- **Tax Deferred**: Traditional IRA, 401(k) or 403(b), Annuities, etc.

- **Tax Free**: Roth IRAs

According to the Retirement Income Certified Professionals (RICP®) program at the American College, retirees should first withdraw money from their taxable accounts—allowing their traditional IRAs and other tax-deferred accounts to compound for as long as possible before drawing on them. The last source from which to draw income is tax free investments like the Roth IRA. The RICP® gives special emphasis to Roths because their growth is not taxable, they have no minimum required distributions, and they carry specific legacy planning benefits.

IRA expert, PBS show host and CPA, Ed Slott comments,

> *Roth IRA distributions to your client's beneficiaries are generally income tax free. And if your client's beneficiary takes a distribution from the inherited Roth IRA after five tax years from the year of your first Roth IRA conversion or tax-year Roth IRA contribution to any Roth IRA, the distribution will be completely income tax and penalty free.*

Clearly having a Roth IRA or converting some your clients' assets to one is a very wise strategy. Let's take a look at what a Roth Conversion did for one couple's retirement.

CASE STUDY: Roth IRA Conversion

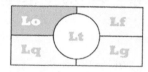

Client Overview: Calvin and Claire (65) are fairly comfortable with their retirement income plan. However, they are somewhat concerned about living longer than they've planned for and the impact future tax rates may have on their savings, should they need to use them, or on their estate should they pass it on.

Financial Position:

- $200,000 Traditional IRA | $400,000 401k/Annuities | $100,000 in Brokerage Account
- $450,000 Home | $50,000 Mortgage | $541/Month Payment

Planning Objective: Convert a portion of Calvin and Claire's tax deferred IRAs into a tax-free Roth IRA for future use, or as an inheritance, while preserving the most amount of principal.

The advisor can begin the Roth Conversion conversation with their clients by exploring three questions:

Do you need the money in your traditional IRA immediately or in the future?
If future, then proceed.

Are you concerned that you may be in a higher tax bracket in the future?
If yes, then proceed.

Do you have the money to pay the taxes on the conversion?
If they are not sure, proceed.

Three Options for Paying the Conversion Taxes

Let's say the taxes to roll over the $200,000 traditional IRA will be $48,000. Your clients have a few choices regarding the accounts they could draw from.

- **They could pay the taxes out of the roll over itself.** Instead of rolling over $200,000, they roll over $152,000, but then they don't receive the full benefit of the transaction.

- **They could take it from their existing IRA or other taxable accounts.** Doing so would mean paying taxes on the IRA distribution as well as incurring the lost opportunity costs from drawing the money early instead of allowing it to continue compounding.

Herein lies the challenge; many people don't have a viable source to pay the conversion taxes, or they need those funds to live on. Simply stated: If you don't have money to pay the tax, you can't convert. However, there is another option.

Use Your Housing Wealth

We know that the majority of older Americans and emerging baby boomers are sitting on a source for paying Roth Conversion taxes: their homes!

How can Housing Wealth be used to pay the taxes for a Roth IRA conversion? The process is easier than you may think.

Step 1: Calculate their HECM benefit. After paying off the $50,000 mortgage on their $450,000 home, the HECM makes a $118,000 line of credit available. www.HecmCalculator.net

Step 2: Determine if they want to pay the taxes all at once, over a 5-year period, or over a 10-year period (for example). If they decide to pay over 5 years, they would draw $9,600 each year from the HECM line of credit. If over 10 years, $4,800 per year.

The charts below demonstrate four things: (1) The growth on the initial line of credit if it were left untouched, (2) the growth on the line of credit if they were to take out $48,000 up front, (3) the growth if they were to take out $9,600 a year over a 5-year period, or (4) the growth if they were to take out $4,800 a year over a 10-year period.

Line of Credit Left Untouched

Age	Beginning of Year Balance	Growth (5%)	End of Year Balance
65	$118,000.00	$5,900.00	$123,900.00
70	$150,601.22	$7,530.06	$158,131.29
75	$192,209.57	$9,610.48	$201,820.04
80	$245,313.53	$12,265.68	$257,579.20
85	$313,089.13	$15,654.46	$328,743.59
90	$399,589.88	$19,979.49	$419,569.38

Line of Credit Growth with One-Time Tax Payment of $48,000 in 1st Year

Age	Beginning of Year Balance	Growth (5%)	Withdrawal	End of Year Balance
65	$118,000.00	$5,900.00	$48,000.00	$75,900.00
70	$92,256.92	$4,612.85	$0	$96,869.77
75	$117,745.81	$5,887.29	$0	$123,633.10
80	$150,276.81	$7,513.84	$0	$157,790.65
85	$191,795.52	$9,589.78	$0	$201,385.30
90	$244,785.09	$12,239.25	$0	$257,024.34

Line of Credit Growth with Taxes Paid Over 5-Year Period

Age	Beginning of Year Balance	Growth (%5)	Withdrawal	End of Year Balance
65	$118,000.00	$5,900.00	$9,600.00	$114,300.00
66	$114,300.00	$5,715.00	$9,600.00	$110,415.00
67	$110,415.00	$5,520.75	$9,600.00	$106,335.75
68	$106,335.75	$5,316.79	$9,600.00	$102,052.54
69	$102,052.54	$5,102.63	$9,600.00	$97,555.16
70	$97,555.16	$4,877.76	$0	$102,432.92
75	$124,507.86	$6,225.39	$0	$130,733.25
80	$158,907.08	$7,945.35	$0	$166,852.44
85	$202,810.18	$10,140.51	$0	$212,950.69
90	$258,842.89	$12,942.14	$0	$271,785.04

Line of Credit Growth with Taxes Paid Over 10-Year Period

Age	Beginning of Year Balance	Growth (%5)	Withdrawal	End of Year Balance
65	$118,000.00	$5,900.00	$4,800.00	$119,100.00
66	$119,100.00	$5,955.00	$4,800.00	$120,255.00
67	$120,255.00	$6,012.75	$4,800.00	$121,467.75
68	$121,467.75	$6,073.39	$4,800.00	$122,741.14
69	$122,741.14	$6,137.06	$4,800.00	$124,078.19
70	$124,078.19	$6,203.91	$4,800.00	$125,482.10
71	$125,482.10	$6,274.11	$4,800.00	$126,956.21
72	$126,956.21	$6,347.81	$4,800.00	$128,504.02
73	$128,504.02	$6,425.20	$4,800.00	$130,129.22
74	$130,129.22	$6,506.46	$4,800.00	$131,835.68
75	$131,835.68	$6,591.78	$0	$138,427.47
80	$168,259.45	$8,412.97	$0	$176,672.42
85	$214,746.43	$10,737.32	$0	$225,483.76
90	$274,076.91	$13,703.85	$0	$287,780.76

Did we meet the planning objective? Convert a portion of Calvin and Claire's tax deferred IRAs into a tax-free Roth IRA for future use, or as an inheritance, while preserving the most amount of principal. I think we did!

By using the HECM to pay all (or even some) of the taxes for the conversion we were able to:

- Convert the entire $200,000 into tax free savings for their retirement needs, or for their heirs.

- Give continued access to HECM Line of Credit even AFTER the conversion.

You may have clients in mind who have considered a Roth Conversion, but have not been able to pay the taxes in a way that makes financial sense. Now, you have another option for them consider – Housing Wealth. Is this worth a conversation?

17

Five Ways Housing Wealth Can Create Unshakable Financial Memories

"True wealth is that which money can't buy, and death can't take away."

– Brent Welch

How do your clients want to be *financially* remembered? This is my working definition of legacy. For some, it is defined by leaving an inheritance after their death. For others, it indicates living a financial life that reflects honor, character, and solid decision making. It may also mean possessing the wherewithal to leave a financial legacy now, while they are still living, and in the future if desired.

How One Man Achieved a Living Legacy

My father, Robert L. Graves, was born in 1926 in Falmouth, Kentucky. He was the oldest of six in a very poor town. His mother, Gracie Graves, had poor eyesight and needed dental work badly. At the time, most dentists would not see my grandmother, and if they would, she couldn't afford their services.

At age fifteen, after completing eighth grade, my father lied about his age and enlisted in the Navy. He wanted to send money home to help his three sisters go to high school (which cost money during that time), but my father's real motivation was to provide eyeglasses and a set of dentures for his mom. He wanted her to feel beautiful and have a sense of pride and dignity.

Upon receiving his first paycheck, he sent money to buy the glasses. His second check went towards a set of teeth. By the time he got home on his first furlough, my grandmother beamed with joy and pride . . . and so did my father. Now, that's legacy, but more on that later.

In this chapter, we will explore several ways that the reverse mortgage can provide a living legacy as well as a traditional one.

CASE STUDY: How to Free Money for Clients to Achieve Legacy Both Now and Later

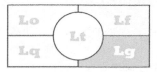

Client Overview: Dennis and Barbara are both seventy years old and have sufficient income to meet their living expenses. They have four children—ages fifty, forty-seven, forty-four, and forty—and ten grandchildren ranging from age eight to twenty-two. They own a $450,000 home with an existing mortgage of $80,000 and will be making a monthly payment of $800 for the next twelve years.

Planning Objective: Help Dennis and Barbara use their existing assets to create a financial legacy for their children and grandchildren now, as well as in the future, without impacting current cash flow or reserves.

By this time, you should know a few basic HECM strategies to help them achieve their planning objective, right?

5 Ways Legacy Can Be Achieved Through Housing Wealth

Based on Dennis and Barbara's ages, the value of their home, and the interest rate at the time, the net HECM will make around $227,900 available to them. From those proceeds, their existing mortgage of $80,000 will be paid off—giving them $800 in additional monthly cash flow. They will also have access to a growing line of credit of $147,900.

HECM REPLACEMENT	
Additional Cash Flow	$800/month
Appreciating Line of Credit	$147,900
Existing Savings	$546,000

The HECM replacement strategy (which should be very familiar at this point) allows us to address other concerns and develop some planning strategies for them. Here are five ways the HECM can enhance the legacy conversation.

1. Legacy Through Long-Term Care Insurance

It's important to note that long-term care planning is not just about insurance; it's about having a comprehensive, realistic plan to address the increasing cost of care in retirement as well as the emotional and financial impact that care could have on families. *This* is the legacy: having the client be proactive in their planning so the emotional burden is not on their families and so they can, where possible, preserve assets from premature erosion and Medicaid seizure.

Since there is such a high likelihood that one or both of a retiring couple will need long-term care, what are the options to offset some of the expenses that it would require?

One option to cover costs is to purchase a traditional **long-term care insurance plan**. The obvious benefits are assuring quality of care for the patient, preventing the assets from either being seized by Medicaid or prematurely depleted, and ensuring the continuation of assets for the remaining spouse or future generations. On the other hand, the premiums for a pure long-term care policy for a seventy-year-old can be very expensive.

If your clients medically qualify for the insurance, how could they replenish the dollars they use for those premiums? They can

repurpose the $800/month they are now saving because of the HECM replacement to meet premium amounts!

Incorporating Housing Wealth to Reduce the Policy Costs

When choosing a traditional long-term care policy, there are four considerations:

($) **The Benefit Amount** (how much per day your policy will pay)

(🕐) **The Benefit Period** (how long that amount will be paid for)

($) **Inflation Protection** (how your benefit amount keeps pace with inflation over time?) and

(🕐) **The Waiting Period** (how long will it take before the policy begins paying)

The Power of Having a Reserve		
YEARS	**LOC**	**TENURE**
0	$147,900	$791
5	$189,680	$1,083
10	$243,428	$1,556
15	$312,405	$2,357
20	$400,928	$3,989
25	$514,535	$8,252

Any adjustment in those four features can have a significant impact in the premium costs. This is where the reverse mortgage can help. Not only can the repurposed mortgage payments cover the premium, but the establishing of the line of credit creates additional options.

For example, the client could choose a lower benefit amount or a shorter benefit period because of the ReLOC. They could use the HECM as an inflation rider also lowering the premiums. (recall chapter 11)

Finally, they could extend the elimination period. During the waiting period, the policy will not pay benefits. If you recover before the waiting period ends, the policy doesn't pay for expenses you incur during the waiting period. The policy pays only for expenses that occur after the waiting period is over. However, the longer the waiting period, the lower the premium for the policy.

You can see that by establishing a HECM line of credit, the client now has flexibility to structure their policy and premium payments to substantially reduce the cost of the coverage.

2. Legacy Through Self-Insuring for Long-Term Care

Although we already covered this conversion strategy in an earlier chapter, it's worth repeating here.

An added benefit of establishing the line of credit is not only that it grows (see chart), but that growth can be converted into full or partial monthly payments at any time in the future.

For Dennis and Barbara, this means that in addition to the $800/month created with the HECM replacement, *they also have other dollars that can be converted in the future and used for legacy planning.*

3. Legacy Through Life Insurance

I once heard a presenter say, "Don't leave your children money; leave them life insurance." For those who can afford to purchase a policy, life insurance provides favorable tax benefits now *and* inheritance benefits when the death benefit is paid.

Life insurance can cover several needs with one single policy. Depending on the policy, you may be able to use it later in retirement to serve as a spending buffer and mitigate some of the risks we've discussed. Newer policies now come with additional "linked" benefits in case money is needed for long-term care coverage.

If a client is healthy enough to qualify, then the biggest issue becomes the price of the premiums, which are more expensive at age sixty-five or seventy than they would have been at forty-five or fifty.

Where do Dennis and Barbara get the money to purchase a life insurance plan without impacting their current cash flow? That's right. The HECM replacement has created $800 per month to pay the premiums. This is getting too easy.

Power Question: If we could create a huge, tax-advantaged inheritance for your children and grandchildren, as well as provide coverage for long-term care or other supplemental resources without impacting your current cash flow, would you want to see how it works?

 ## Legacy Through Life Insurance for Children

It's typically between ages forty and fifty-five that people begin thinking about life insurance. The thought of leaving their spouse and children without sufficient means is very sobering, and though many policies are obtained in those years, many more are not. Work, busyness, or the price of the premiums during the child-rearing years are often prohibitive.

One of the vehicles your clients can use to help is the **purchase of a life insurance policy for their children**. If done correctly, the policy will not only provide a death benefit for the kids, but also a life benefit in the form of policy loans for the retirees themselves (should they need it in the future).

Maybe their children have enough money to purchase life insurance but not enough to obtain a certain amount of coverage. Mom and Dad can provide some "legacy now" benefits by using their "liberated" income or line of credit conversion to cover the premium costs.

Dennis and Barbara even have the ability to purchase a policy for their grandchildren. For a very low price, they can buy a policy that builds cash value and then converts when the grandchildren reach adulthood. Imagine giving each of your grandchildren a cash value life insurance policy available when they became adults. Now, there's a "legacy now" strategy!

4. Legacy Through Education

In today's world, most understand that education is key to long-term financial success. This doesn't always mean college (as per Bill Gates or Steve Jobs), but for most it does. At a minimum, it means a quality high school education.

Sallie Mae, the financial intermediary tasked with student loan servicing, says that about 5 percent of college costs are currently being paid by relatives such as grandparents. Dr. James Johnston of SAGE Scholars/Tuition Rewards says that at many of the smaller, private colleges in the U.S., the average monthly parent/grandparent contribution is from $1,300 to $1,500.

Here's the point: because Dennis and Barbara have an additional $800 per month in cash flow, as well as $147,000 in a growing/convertible line of credit, they are well-positioned to become their own grant-making entity, or low-interest student loan organization. They can help pay for tuition and books, offer loans, or even pay a portion of their grandchildren's student loans. What a legacy!

5. Legacy Through Lapsed Policy Prevention

There are many ways to use insurance to meet legacy and estate-planning goals, but those goals cannot be achieved if premiums cannot be maintained as clients age. What is the point of having long-term care insurance or life insurance if they can't pay the premiums when they need them most? Having a reserve and/or excess cash flow allows them to have premium-replacement dollars if anything were to happen to their income.

More Than "Just" Money

After the Navy, my dad married my mom, had children, and set out on a quest for a better life. He moved the family, acquired—and kept—good jobs, rose in rank, and ascended the career ladder. He required all four of his children to go to school and college, hold a job, save our money, pay bills on time, give generously, and read widely. And that's what all four of us did.

My father did not leave me much in terms of money ($3,500 and a pocket knife), but I used the money he did leave to buy bubble gum machines that started me on my first entrepreneurial adventure and set the tone for my life. Truly what my father left me is worth more than money; he instilled a biblical legacy of honoring your mother and father, a work legacy of doing the right thing, and a financial legacy of relentlessness. My father passed to me a baton of true wealth that money didn't buy and death can't steal.

Asking your clients questions about the type of financial legacy they want to leave can be a highly revealing conversation that puts their priorities in the right light.

The HECM is a creative source to helping materialize their desires. Be sure to include it in the conversation.

18

Seven HECM Strategies That Benefit Women

In an earlier chapter, I gave five reasons that there can be no significant retirement income planning conversation without giving special consideration to the uniqueness of planning for women (wives in particular).

As we close out our Case Studies section, I want to bring to your attention a few HECM strategies that, I believe, have greater relevance for women than men. The first few I will simply highlight, since they have already been covered. I will expand upon the last two: Social Security and Gray Divorce.

1. Paying Off a Mortgage

Nothing is more concerning to retirees than carrying debt into their retirement years. The sad fact is that consumer and housing debt will eat up a very large portion of the modern retiree's monthly income and peace of mind.

This concern is magnified for the married woman due to the near-certain income reduction that she will experience at the death of her spouse. Having the HECM Replacement or Exchange conversation (chapters 12 and 14) is a way to alleviate some of her future concerns.

2. Creating an Income Replacement Strategy

Similarly, because the income for most women will be adjusted at the death of their spouse (e.g. life insurance, pension selections), an established HECM can often supplement needed income.

To optimize the amount of income the HECM could replace, a wise strategy may be to establish it as a line of credit early in retirement and let it grow as a type of **income replacement insurance**. It can be used bi-directionally or converted to monthly income if the loan is still in force.

Having this conversation early can ease the mind of wives as well as single women who desire a buffer asset to hedge against market volatility.

Additionally, many pension systems are hurting and in danger of collapse. At the very least, they are being restructured, so that employees must now pay for medical expenses. A recent *Forbes* article said nearly one million U.S. workers and retirees are currently covered by pension plans on the verge of collapse. Establishing a standby HECM line of credit could serve as a much-needed lifeline.

3. Creating a Long-Term Care Plan

In an earlier chapter, I mentioned that nearly 70 percent of Americans will need some sort of long-term care during their lifetimes, with the average length of care being nearly three years. Thirty percent of the primary caregivers are over the age of sixty-five. Oftentimes, both the literal and figurative heavy lifting of caregiving falls on the wife, and it is typically she who will suffer the indignity of having someone else care for her. This is a gloomy, often overlooked reality that weighs heavily on females.

Using housing wealth to help create a long-term care plan is very wise; having a plan is better than having none, especially for women!

4. Life Insurance

A very simple way to help the longer-living spouse is to establish or maintain life insurance that can fulfill a variety of functions upon the death of the first spouse, as well as legacy benefits at the passing of the second. For pennies on the dollar, retirees can establish a policy or set up a reserve fund to ensure there is enough to finance the rest of retirement.

5. Right Size with HECM for Purchase

Even though the house may become too large and expenses burdensome, the value of homeownership is still important to many retirees. This often happens when funds are tight in later years. Perhaps a sickness drains savings or the husband dies and the home, though cherished, is too large to maintain on the current income. Using the HECM for Purchase (chapter 15) allows the client to purchase her next home for around 50 to 60 percent down and have no monthly mortgage payments. For wives/widows and caregivers, this could be a real blessing.

6. Social Security and Retirement Income Optimization

One of the most significant ways to optimize retirement outcomes is to have a very simple conversation regarding Social Security. (The principle can be applied to pensions, IRAs, 401k and annuities, too.)

The system is constructed in a way that offers flexibility; you can begin taking retirement benefits anywhere between age sixty and seventy. You get 100 percent of your benefits at your full retirement age. If you take it early, you get less, and if you wait, you get more.

Below is a very common chart produced by the Social Security Administration that shows a person getting $1,000 at full retirement age. If they take it early at sixty-two, they get much less than if they take it at age seventy. Most advisors already know this, though many clients still do not, or they may not fully understand the impact.

The prevailing wisdom states that you should take your Social Security as early as possible if these three things are true of you:

- You are the lowest *aggregate* wage earner. Historically, this has been women in the marriage. There may have been years when she made more money than her husband, but over their work career, the woman is typically the lower total wage earner. When that is the case, taking *her* social security benefits at age sixty-two is okay.

Social Security and Retirement Income Optimization

Monthly Benefit Amount by Age you Decide to Start Receiving Benefits
This example assumes a benefit of $1,000 at a full retirement age of 66

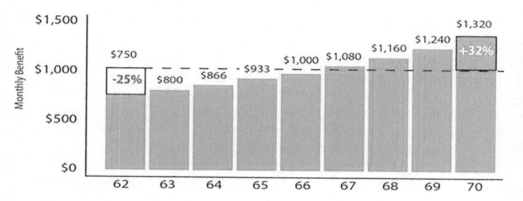

- You are expected to live fewer years than the *average* person. For the most part, Social Security benefits are actuarially balanced. This means you gain no more or less if you defer, as long as you die "on time."

Most charts show the breakeven point as seventy-nine years of age. If you started taking your money early and died prior to seventy-nine, you won. One drawback with using life expectancy to plan for retirement is that it's just an average. One-half will die before life expectancy, and the other half after. So how many of your clients are average?

Updated charts suggest that a married man who has reached sixty-five will live on average another eighteen years, and a woman another twenty plus. The society of actuaries says there is a 25 percent chance that a sixty-five-year-old man will live to ninety-three, and a 25 percent chance that a sixty-five-year-old woman will live to ninety-six. For a couple, sixty-five-years-old, there's a 25 percent chance that the surviving spouse lives to ninety-eight. Considering this, planning for your clients to live past seventy-nine may be a wise discussion to have.

- You don't have a better alternative. This is the third reason to take Social Security early. The truth is, this is the case for the majority of people who start their Social Security at age sixty-two. Many leave work earlier than expected, cannot get other employment, or have no other means (that they know of) to defer. What are they to do?

A Simple Potential Solution:

A client can defer by establishing a HECM line of credit at the onset of retirement and then drawing from it to sup- plement all or a portion of what Social Security provides. The non-taxable dollars from the HECM can be used to defer Social Security or a pension. It can also be used to help clients wait longer before getting an annuity or taking their IRA's before the required age of seventy and a half,

- allowing them to grow. Deferring seven years also shortens their retirement draw period. When done correctly, this can significantly increase the probability of retirement success.

The scope of this conversation will not be covered here, but I do unpack more in the certification course.

7. Gray Divorce and Silver Solutions

In an article entitled "Gray Divorce Boosts Poverty Level for Women," financial author Mary Beth Franklin shares about the growing phenomenon of gray divorce and how women are par- ticularly impacted by it. Here are a few excerpts:

- Divorce among spouses age fifty and older is increasingly common and has negative implications for baby boomers' retirement security.

- Even though the overall U.S. divorce rate has remained sta- ble since 1990, *gray divorce has doubled* during that period.

- The percentage of baby boomers living in poverty is *nearly five times higher among unmarried* (19 percent) than married (4 percent).

- Gray divorce appears to diminish wealth more than earlier divorce.

- In addition, gender matters and economic disparity between men and women widens with age. A whopping 27 percent of gray divorced women are poor, compared to just 11 percent of gray divorced men. *Women are impacted in a greater measure than men are.*

As noted in the article, these types of divorces were rare in times past, but this is no longer the case, and more are predicted with the advent of the baby boomers. Divorce is always painful, but if there is a home involved, there may some solutions to create a real win/win, especially for women.

Below is an example of how a bad situation was made better by the presence of a reverse mortgage.

CASE STUDY: Gray Divorce and Silver Solutions

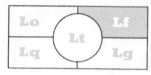

Client Overview: Betty and John Simkins (ages seventy and seventy-one) never imagined their marriage would fail. After forty-five years together, they have three grown children with several grandchildren who live nearby Their home of forty years has appreciated to around $400,000.

The divorce decree has stipulated that any remaining home equity is to be divided equally, but Betty wants to remain in the home, and John wants to move out and get on with his new life and girlfriend. What can be done?

Four Options:

Option 1: Sell and Go Their Separate Ways

The home is sold for $400,000 and the proceeds divided. Betty and John each get $200,000 to go and start over. The possibilities? A rental situation, a smaller home, or a larger home with a monthly mortgage payment.

Option 2: Buy Out with Traditional Refinance

Betty decides to buy John out. She obtains a traditional refinance for $200,000 and gives that cash to John. Betty keeps the house and now has a monthly mortgage payment for the next twenty to thirty years.

Option 3: Take Out a HECM and Stay

Betty gets a reverse mortgage on the existing home. The HECM makes available around $200,000. Betty gives that money to her ex-husband. Now she can *stay in the home without any mortgage payments required.*

Option 4: HECM for Purchase

The home is sold, and Betty takes her $200,000 payout. She wants to purchase a home for $300,000, but she does not want to have a traditional mortgage with monthly payments. She also does not want to pull $100,000 from her savings.

Her advisor told her she can use the HECM for Purchase program to move into the $300,000 home for around $144,000 down, have no monthly mortgage payments, preserve her savings, and still have $56,000 left over from her divorce settlement.

The chart below shows she could also move into a $375,000 home or $200,000 home and save more money.

Divorces are always unpleasant, but they are especially problematic for women. These seven HECM strategies provide powerful means to assist women in the planning process. The conversations

Proceeds from Sale	New Home Price	HECM Proceeds	Down Payment	Liberated Proceeds
$200,000	$300,000	$144,000	$156,000	$44,000
$200,000	$375,000	$180,000	$195,000	$5,000
$200,000	$200,000	$96,000	$104,000	$96,000

are best when broached early, but even when appropriately implemented and coordinated with other assets later in the game, they can be a real-life changer.

SECTION 4:

INCORPORATING HOME EQUITY INTO YOUR PRACTICE

Common Strategies to Implement Housing Wealth into Your Practice

19

Can Advisors Make Money with Housing Wealth Legally, Ethically, Morally, and Compliantly?

Can reverse mortgages help me keep more assets under management?

My compliance department would rather me not talk about reverse mortgages. How should I handle that?

Can advisors earn a commission for referring a reverse mortgage? What if I got my license and originated the loans myself?

Certainly, there are some legal and compliance barriers to using reverse mortgages. What are the best rules of thumb to follow in exploring these with my clients?

I recently received an email from a financial wholesaler who didn't believe that reverse mortgages had any practical value for the advisors his team served. As you may have gathered, I often find questions to be a more powerful tool than simply spelling out the answer, so I responded with these three questions:

1. What if the advisors you serve were able to do $100,000 more *in additional annuity business* each month? Would they want to know how?

2. What if they could do *one additional life or long-term care policy with a $500 a month premium?* Would they want to see how?

3. What if they could *preserve more of their client assets under management longer* without having to ask the client to cut back on their current lifestyle? Would that make a difference in their practice?

Many advisors have this same sentiment. They might phrase it differently, but it all comes down to the same thing: Does incorporating housing wealth into my practice help my bottom line?

Four Ways Advisors Are Compensated

I'm often asked if an advisor can earn a commission or be paid a fee for originating or referring a reverse mortgage. The simple answers are yes *and* no. Before I explain this, let's explore how advisors are generally compensated, so we can better understand how reverse mortgages seamlessly integrate with the four ways advisors make money.

 ### The Money You Manage

For advisors who manage investments, helping your clients' savings last as long as they live is a key challenge. One of the most common dangers to their savings accounts is asset erosion (often due to inflation), premature or ill-timed withdrawals, or simply beginning their retirement at the wrong time and experiencing sequence of returns risk.

Building a volatility buffer—a reverse mortgage strategy we will discuss later—can be an efficient way to mitigate the more common risks of retirement and avoid premature asset erosion. By implementing the concepts you'll find in the case studies, you will learn how to effectively keep more assets under management longer, leading to greater retirement outcomes and tremendous client satisfaction that you would not otherwise be able to achieve apart from the reverse mortgage.

The Products You Sell

Annuities, life insurance, and long-term and linked benefits insurance all have their place in a comprehensive retirement income plan, and they all require clients to have either a lump sum of cash or a stream of dollars to fund the premiums. Where can an advisor find clients with both?

The benefit of understanding and incorporating reverse mortgages in your client conversations is that it will give you the strategies to identify existing and new clients who have access to cash and income to fund premiums, without ever using the proceeds of a reverse mortgage to accomplish it!

The last two ways advisors generate revenue are often overlooked but remain essential to maintain a long-term, profitable practice.

 ## The Clients You Keep

Competition among advisors is fierce, and client attrition can pose a danger even for the most experienced advisor. Keeping your clients engaged and encouraged is one way to retain them. Another is helping them use the assets they already have to create greater retirement security.

When an advisor helps a client create cash flow, reduce risks, insure assets, increase liquidity, or add new dollars back into savings, that advisor becomes invaluable, and their client loyalty goes through the roof.

The People Your Clients Tell

When clients are satisfied or even stunned by what their advisors have accomplished, they'll gladly share their retirement success story with their friends and family. As I mentioned earlier, only 16 percent of baby boomers have a written financial plan. Opportunity is ripe for advisors to serve this aging population by helping them optimize their retirement income plans.

A Tale of Two Advisors: When Knowledge Gained is Revenue Earned

Let's focus on two advisors, both of whom represent the same products and carriers. They both visit the same sixty-two-year-old, married couple; one goes in the morning and the other in the afternoon. The clients identify themselves as having $300,000 in an investment account and $150,000 in cash, CDs and money markets. They are looking for better retirement outcomes without too much risk or exposure.

The first advisor meets with the clients and leaves with nothing. The second advisor shares the same company and carrier stories, brochures and presentations, but she leaves with $50,000 to be added to the assets under management, a $100,000 policy for fixed income, a 1035 exchange for an old annuity, and a life insurance contract. Same clients, same products and presentations, but two very different results.

What was the difference? The variance was the second advisor knew the questions, concepts, stories, and strategies to incorporate housing wealth into the dialogue, while the first advisor did not. Furthermore, she was able to accomplish what she did without using the proceeds of the reverse mortgage. She served her client in a way that was legally, ethically, morally, and responsibly as a fiduciary, as well as 100 percent compliant.

Here's another instance in which housing wealth makes a big difference. A client with a $500,000 portfolio has a current withdrawal rate that will cause the plan to be exhausted in less than seventeen years. One advisor implements a traditional conservation/reallocation strategy that requires the client to make lifestyle reductions, and the savings are prolonged by five years.

The second advisor implements a housing wealth strategy (see section three) that requires no behavioral modifications, and the client's savings last over thirty years. Which wealth manager more significantly impacted their client's retirement outcomes and, by default, kept more assets under management longer?

When a Client Asks About a Reverse Mortgage

It's already been stated that to generate revenue in conjunction with housing wealth, you must be able to incorporate it into planning conversations. Below are a few ways I've heard advisors respond when their clients brought up reverse mortgages. One is good; three are unacceptable.

 "I am hearing interesting things about them and learning more." This is a response of **balance** and music to my ears. It's fair, responsible, and allows the dialogue between and advisor and client to continue.

 "I don't know anything about reverse mortgages." This is a response of **ignorance**. I use the term in its original sense: "to be without the proper information." Sometimes an advisor simply does not know very much about reverse mortgages.

 "I would never tell my clients to do one of those." I affectionally term this response as one of **arrogance**. Over the last twenty years, I have found this predisposition one of the toughest with which to reason. These advisors have positioned themselves as the custodian of knowledge and are willing to dispense that knowledge whether they have updated and revised information or not.

On occasion, you will find a public television broadcast or a popular author telling their audience that the last thing they would ever tell a client to do is a reverse mortgage. It's possible you held that position prior to reading this far in this book, but I hope that by this point, your perception is changing.

 "I can't talk about reverse mortgages." Out of all the responses so far, this one is the most reactionary and painful to me. It is rooted in negligence. In every other profession, a similar response would be intolerable.

Imagine going to the oncologist and receiving test results that reveal you have stage-two cancer. As you inquire about various treatment options, you mention radiation and your doctor says, "The hospital doesn't allow me to talk about that." It would be stunning. Perhaps you could understand if you spoke about some treatment plan that was experimental and not widely accepted, but radiation for cancer?

Clearly, I am passionate about this subject. I understand how the "we can't talk about it" position evolved, but what I cannot understand is why that position continues, especially in light of the evidence of the HECM's usefulness in retirement income planning.

How Did Reverse Mortgages Fall Out of Favor with Compliance Folks?

The short history is that reverse mortgages and annuities were first cousins. When I started in this business, you could go to the AARP website and get a quote for a reverse mortgage lump sum, line of credit, monthly payment, and a single premium immediate annuity all in the same printout. As annuity interest rates declined, the quoting functions ceased. This gave rise to equity indexed annuities. The early products had big commissions and long surrender periods.

During that period, a few advisors got overzealous and, against wise counsel and warning, suggested their clients get a reverse mortgage lump sum, then dump 100% of the benefits into the purchase of certain annuity products and, on occasion, some equities.

The problem during that time was not that the annuities were bad but that advisors were counseled to leave the client with plenty of liquidity, usually being advised never to put more than 50% of the proceeds into any product.

It only took two advisors, one in Portland, Maine, and the other in Washington State to become greedy. This was discovered, and what was previously known as the National Association of Securities Dealers (NASD) issued a decree that none of their advisors could talk about reverse mortgages. Other entities followed suit, and thus, the season of prohibition began.

The concern of compliance officers is not unwarranted; it's just *outdated*. Beginning in 2011, MetLife's mature market institute began to look at reverse mortgages as a viable retirement planning tool. In 2012, the Funding Longevity Task Force was formed, the first publication in the Journal of Financial Planning was published, and by October 2013, FINRA had officially changed their written position on reverse mortgages to be affirmative.

How to Navigate Compliance/Broker-Dealer Obstacles

What happens if your compliance department doesn't want you to speak about reverse mortgages; what can you do? Over the years, I have discovered that reasonable compliance departments want to make sure that advisors primarily avoid the following three practices when it comes to reverse mortgages.

1. **Don't use the proceeds for any investments**. The Securities and Exchange Commission already has regulations about taking the proceeds of a loan and purchasing equities. Using the proceeds from a reverse mortgage to purchase equities is not an acceptable practice and is filled with ethical dilemmas.

   There are some, however, who would like to use proceeds to purchase a fixed or deferred income annuity. Though not expressly forbidden, I have found in times past that this practice leads to greed, unsuitable product placement, and loss of liquidity for retirees. I would agree with compliance departments that this practice is not a suitable way to use the proceeds of a reverse mortgage.

2. **Don't accept any commission or fee.** For many under the auspices of a compliance department, nothing sings conflict of interest like the exchange of monies. Most elite advisors understand this and have no problem with this restriction.

3. **Don't endorse, recommend, or speak about the product specifics**. Just as an advisor cannot give tax advice or legal counsel unless they are licensed to do so, they cannot speak

about the rates, fees, or terms of a reverse mortgage without holding that license.

I will take this a step further and suggest that advisors not give a whole-hearted endorsement or recommendation of a specific reverse mortgage program or product. This is because the program "specifics" are always evolving and changing. This book suggests you understand and integrate *housing wealth* as part of a comprehensive financial plan.

In the next chapter, I provide a simple disclosure for advisors to use that explains their position on reverse mortgages and meets the compliance concerns as outlined in this chapter.

Question: What does an advisor do or say if their clients have glaring tax inefficiencies? Or if they have legal gaps or don't have sufficient liability insurance on their property? What would an advisor say or do?

Answer: They would share with their clients that they have some tax, legal, or insurance risk inefficiencies that might affect their retirement. They would recommend that they seek the advice of an attorney, tax advisor, or property/casualty specialist. They might speak about other clients who employed a certain tax strategy or incorporated a type of will or trust. They may discuss the value of liability insurance. They might point them toward a licensed reverse mortgage professional who could help them unlock their housing wealth and protect their savings. Any of those would be appropriate and expected of any advisor who is looking out for the best interests of their clients.

What would be considered strange, unprofessional, and generally frowned upon is if the advisor saw these gaps, knew of potential solutions and strategies that could help, but refused to speak up or were told that they could not say anything. This response exposes not only the advisor but their compliance departments to scrutiny and possible litigation.

The Real Legal Danger You Face

The road forward is pretty simple; once you finish this book, it will be clear as day. The greater danger for compliance departments and advisors is not in "playing it safe," but rather in failing to recognize that housing wealth has been proven mathematically and scientifically to improve retirement outcomes and efficiency for a large number of retirees. Not incorporating it would be like the cancer treatment hospital telling their oncologists that they can't talk about all treatment options!

Nine Things Compliance Needs to Know About Reverse Mortgages

If you find yourself in the compliance department (or wish to enlighten others within your organization), here are a few things you should know about reverse mortgages:

1. Reverse mortgages are no longer a product of last resort. FINRA reversed their "last resort" position in 2014.

2. The DOL Best Interest of Care Standard requires advisors to have a cursory knowledge of retirement resources that can impact their clients.

3. Having advisors say nothing about reverse mortgages is irresponsible given the research over the last four years. Saying nothing is dangerous for you and your advisors if clients learn you have not been upfront about all opportunities.

4. Having advisors say the wrong thing about reverse mortgages is as bad as saying nothing.

5. Getting certified in reverse mortgages/housing wealth is simple and will give advisors the skills they need to speak about the resource as part of a comprehensive planning process. More information can be found at www.HecmInstitute.com

6. Most major thought leaders and academic institutions have embraced reverse mortgages.

7. The current retirement income crisis demands more tools.

8. Nearly 100 percent of retirees have already seen, read, heard of, or inquired about reverse mortgages and expect their advisors to have a basic understanding of the subject matter.

9. Advisors already have a team to handle other aspects of their clients' retirements. Having a qualified housing wealth consultant as part of that comprehensive team is no different.

Can Advisors Get Paid for Transacting Reverse Mortgages?

Back to the pertinent question: **can an advisor be paid a referral fee or earn a commission for reverse mortgages?**

No, an advisor cannot be paid a referral fee for simply sending a client to a qualified reverse mortgage loan professional (this is a violation of the Real Estate Serving Procedures Act), but **yes,** an advisor can be paid for transacting a reverse mortgage loan.

To do so, an advisor needs to either a) become an employee of a federally chartered banking institution or b) pass a National Mortgages Licensing Services (NMLS) proficiency test, pass the state-specific test, obtain a sponsor, and register with the United States government as a loan originator. Either of these ways allows advisors to earn a legal commission.

Although advisors *can* become loan originators—and several of my advisor friends have at one time or another pursued this—my strong recommendation after twenty years of practice is that they focus on using the skills they have spent years honing and allow those who specialize in reverse mortgages to assist them in helping existing clients and identifying new ones. I have found that advisors who focus on their craft but have a network of specialists to call as needed tend to not only be the most successful in serving their clients but also generate the most revenue.

Another question that sometimes arises: **Can advisors use the direct proceeds from a reverse mortgage to purchase an annuity, equity, mutual fund, or some other investment?**

The short answer is that your clients can choose to do whatever they want with the proceeds of their reverse mortgage. However, nearly all insurers, broker dealers, state banking and insurance commissioners, and organizations such as FINRA, the SEC, both houses of Congress, and the CFPB have shown tremendous concern when advisors take the direct proceeds of a reverse mortgage and invest them in annuities or equities.

I have learned that this is not necessary for advisors who understand how housing wealth works.

Okay, Don, so if an advisor cannot earn a fee, should not become NMLS licensed, and cannot use the direct proceeds to purchase an annuity or equity product, how then does an advisor make money?

Mini Case Study: How Housing Wealth Revealed New Income Opportunities

Earlier in this chapter, I spoke about the sixty-two-year-old couple who had $300,000 in investments and $150,000 in CDs and money markets. They were looking for better retirement outcomes without too much risk or exposure. One advisor was unable to help, but the other was able to help and at the same time increase her revenue. What was the difference?

The difference was that the second advisor understood a few housing wealth principles.

HOUSING WEALTH

Client's Home: $400,000 | Mortgage Balance: $60,000 | Monthly Payment: $550

The client obtained a HECM that provided $160,000 in benefit. This paid off the $60,000 mortgage and freed up $550 in monthly payments for the next fifteen years. Additionally, the HECM provided a $100,000 reserve that grew at 5 percent.

ADVISOR ENGAGEMENT

√ The client's **liquidity concern** is met with the use of the ReLOC. Now they can reposition **$100,000** of the $150,000 they held into vehicles that have better yields. They can retain $50,000 in liquidity with the money market and rely on the $100,000 in liquidity with the ReLOC.

√ The **$550** of **liberated mortgage payment** dollars can now be used as premium replacement dollars for a life insurance policy with a long-term care rider.

√ The investment account remains preserved from premature erosion (and even strengthened).

You see the difference? Housing wealth is an integrative, knowledge-based strategy designed to change retirement outcomes. The advisor who incorporates this will find sufficient opportunity to preserve assets and generate additional revenue in ways that are legal, ethical, moral, and compliant without ever having to use the direct proceeds of the HECM to accomplish it.

The question is: **How many additional clients per month could you help with these strategies? What impact could this have on your practice?**

Reverse mortgages are no longer some rogue, vague, or obscure financial treatment but rather a proven cure for many of the retirement challenges that are facing existing retirees and emerging baby boomers.

Incorporating housing wealth as part of a comprehensive retirement planning conversation is no longer optional. It is essential!

20

Five Ways to Implement Housing Wealth into Your Practice

If you've read this far, then you are already full of ideas, concepts, and strategies for implementing housing wealth in your practice. I bet you've already identified clients whom this could benefit. You may have even practiced some of the sample conversations covered in the chapters. You've certainly seen the three fundamental ways reverse mortgages have changed the retirement income conversation:

- They've changed the way advisors **SEE** the housing asset.

- They've changed the way advisors **SOLVE** the five most pressing retirement concerns.

- They've changed the way advisors **SEAMLESSLY** incorporate housing wealth into planning.

Now, I trust that you have caught the vision and are dreaming big. In that regard, this final section will be short. I want to share four simple ways to implement these principles, eliminate the guesswork, and help you move forward quickly.

1. Practice the Five Conversations

In chapter 5, we discussed the five most important conversations advisors can have with their clients. We have used those conversations throughout this book and built our case studies around them. Those five conversations and their subsequent questions are foundational and should be internalized by advisors.

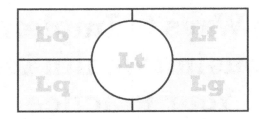

When should you use them? In my experience, there are three interactions where clients are the most open to exploring their concerns with their advisor.

Initial Meeting: Imagine you have been introduced to new clients, and you are sitting down with them for the first time. I am confident that you already have your fact finder and questionnaire ready, but I encourage you to incorporate some of the five core concerns language into that time, especially when the conversation turns to their current home and any monthly payments they may have.

 Suggestion: Start getting comfortable with using the words home equity, housing wealth, the home equity conversion mortgage, and HECM's. Reverse mortgages are like that 1997 cell phone, remember?

Client Review Meetings: Many advisors have regularly scheduled meetings with their clients where they review their portfolio and make necessary adjustments. These are powerful times to share the 5L concerns and discuss how housing wealth is changing retirement income planning. Remember the simple question you learned previously: "{Insert client name}, what would retirement be like if you didn't have to make a monthly mortgage payment?"

Regardless of how they answer, you have a potential solution in your toolbox!

 Suggestion: Try practicing the discussion with a colleague. Have them pretend to be the client. The more you get used to the framework, the more comfortable your conversation will be when it's game time.

Troubleshooting Meetings: The third common meeting is when the clients call in with a question or concern. No doubt that concern will be related to one of the 5Ls. You can also think in terms of the five challenges housing wealth addresses to determine if they need increased cash flow, protection from risks, the ability to preserve what they have, liquidity for spending shocks, or the addition of new dollars into savings.

 Suggestion: Have something at your phone—a note or checklist perhaps—to jog your memory. Or think of your hand as you grab the receiver; for each of your fingers, there is a housing wealth opportunity.

When it comes down to it, housing wealth gives you the ability to have planning conversations where you thought none existed. I encourage you to complete the following steps:

- Assemble a list of clients, age sixty-two or over, who own a house and might be a good fit for housing wealth opportunities.

- Based on notes from previous meetings, write what you think may be each client's major concern of the 5Ls.

- Decide, on a client-by-client basis, if their needs warrant an in-person meeting or can be addressed in a phone call.

- Prep your teammates, if they will be assisting you. Explain what involvement you expect from them and, at minimum, provide them with a summary of the 5Ls. (Better yet, gift them a copy of this book to review before the meetings.)

- Know the next steps for clients who are interested in moving forward. If this involves referring them to a reverse mortgage specialist, have that person's contact information handy.

- Keep an open mind and be prepared to discover new ways to brighten your clients' retirement outcomes!

2. Provide Educational Resources

One of the easiest ways to continue the housing wealth conversation is by providing your clients with educational materials that explain how the tool is being used by others. I suggest finding articles and publications from third-party sources that your clients would recognize: *Forbes, Investment News, The Wall Street Journal,* The American College, Boston College, MIT, etc.

By providing materials, you are showing the value that education and information has on creating quality retirement income strategies. We have a list of educational resources that could fill that need at http://www.HECMAdvisorsGroup.com/Resources

Remember, your job is not to push, promote, or endorse; it is to educate your clients on the tools that can possibly help their retirement outcomes.

 Suggestion: Having third-party articles on hand will also show your clients that you've done your homework—increasing their confidence in you.

In consideration of the DOL ruling, it may be beneficial to have your clients acknowledge that you've offered education about reverse mortgages. The following is an excerpt from a memo of understanding that we created for advisors. You may download this from the resources page at www.HECMAdvisorsGroup.com/Resources *Please note that this is not a legally binding document and should be reviewed by your lawyers before use.*

Memo of Understanding

The HECM/Housing Wealth Conversation

As an advisor, I have a fiduciary responsibility to do what is in the best interest of my clients. Part of that responsibility means staying informed about current thoughts, trends, and legitimate resources that could have a positive or negative effect upon my ability to help my clients meet their retirement goals.

For the last several years, the Home Equity Conversion Mortgage (HECM), or reverse mortgage, has grown in popularity, and recent research suggests that its appropriate and strategic use may be helpful in positively impacting retirement outcomes.

As an advisor, I have come to believe that in order to engage in (or review for you) a thorough and comprehensive financial plan, the housing asset cannot be ignored if certain desired retirement outcomes and protections are to be achieved.

By no means do we suggest that a HECM is right for every client, but we (along with the recent academic research) acknowledge the importance of the housing asset being part of the retirement planning conversation.

In 2014, the Financial Industry Regulatory Agency (FINRA) noted that the Department of Housing and Urban Development (HUD) had recently made changes to Home Equity Conversion Mortgages (HECM's). In response, they stated:

> "We are reissuing this alert to reiterate that while reverse mortgages can help seniors manage their finances if used responsibly, they come with costs and risks. We urge homeowners thinking about reverse mortgages to make informed decisions and carefully weigh all of their options before proceeding. And, if you do decide a reverse mortgage is right for you, be sure to make prudent use of your loan." – FINRA 2014

Reverse mortgages are not an approved product of _____ or _____ Advisors. We are not authorized to discuss rates, terms, fees or any other matters specific to the HECM loan. For this, we suggest that you seek the counsel of a qualified home equity retirement income professional.

Should you choose to obtain a HECM, neither _____ nor _____ Advisors will share in the loan origination fee or be compensated in any way by the lender and/or its subsidiaries, agents, or affiliates.

We acknowledge and agree that the proceeds of the Home Equity Conversion Mortgage will not be used to invest in any financial product through _____ or _____ Advisors, its subsidiaries, agents, partners, or affiliates.

3. Host a Workshop, Seminar, or Webinar

In 2017, the National Council on Aging did a study of reverse mortgages and found that the majority of retirees overwhelmingly favored the benefits of the program to a traditional loan, but when asked why they hadn't done one, their common response was that *they did not know anyone whom they could trust.*

Hosting a seminar and bringing in a third-party speaker allows you to be the hero! After all, you discovered a solution that you're now sharing with others. You prove to be a thought leader—a caring advisor who has searched the earth for all legitimate, retirement-enhancing tools.

Another reason third-party workshops are beneficial is that advisors don't have to present on something that they are not qualified to explain in depth. They can have others who understand retirement income discuss how a client's income, investments, insurance, and annuities, combined with housing wealth, can work together to help create greater retirement outcomes.

A live workshop can provide that, but in this digital age, streaming the workshop, offering the video replay, and/or adding the media to your website can do this as well, and on a long-term basis. Whichever way you choose, make sure your clients get the reverse mortgage information from you and not an actor, postcard, or another advisor's cold call.

Does This Really Work?

A few years ago, I had an advisor ask how he could get information to his clients without having the stigma of the "reverse mortgage" taint the conversation before it started. I told him that 99 percent of emerging boomers and existing retirees have already seen, read, heard, or inquired about reverse mortgages, and the majority have a positive opinion. I assured him that what his clients were most concerned about was *his* opinion of reverse mortgages.

I asked him to conduct a little experiment. When he was meeting with clients, weave this statement into the conversation: "I recently attended a seminar on reverse mortgages hosted by a college professor." Then stop! Don't say anything else. Just wait and see what the clients say. I can promise you that most will look to his expression to see what they should say next.

The advisor tried this experiment—holding his tongue. He found that his clients would sheepishly say, "Well, what do you think about them?" At this point, the door has been opened; he can now share some of the things he learned.

After helping about twenty clients in this way, he realized he was on to something and invited me in for a workshop. He thought about twenty of his clients would register, but sixty-nine did. They brought their friends, neighbors, and children. It turned out to be a huge win/win for him and his clients.

4. Partner with the Right Professional

If I told you that all auto mechanics are the same, what would you say? How about plumbers, dentists, attorneys . . . or advisors? They may all have the same resources at their disposal, but they certainly do not have the same skill or character.

From the nearly twenty years I have been involved with HECMs, I can certainly tell you that all lenders are not the same. The product itself does not change, but the skill, knowledge, and application of the one practicing it does. (Think about it: just having milk, butter, eggs, flour, sugar, baking powder, and vanilla on the table does not mean you know how to make a good cake.)

I urge you to partner with HECM professionals who are specifically trained in retirement income principles and know how to speak your language and support your practice. The following are answers to a few common questions you and/or your clients may now have.

"Should I shop around for the best price?"

In my experience, the cheapest price does not always equal the *lowest cost* or *best choice* (see chapter 9). Pricing for reverse mortgages is not dramatically different from one lender to the next, but experience and competency certainly are!

"How do I know if I've found the right lender?"

I recommend finding a Lending Partner who is:

- Skilled and specialized in reverse mortgages.

- Retirement-income focused and housing-wealth certified.

- Program and proceeds agnostic. This means they get paid the same commission whether your client draws out a large amount up front or establishes a line of credit and draws nothing. This type of lender is not always available, and therefore, this requirement is not a deal-breaker, but you should be aware if a lender suggests that your client take out any additional upfront dollars from the HECM that are not required or part of a plan.

Visit www.HecmInstitute.com to see more recommendations.

5. Become a Certified Housing Wealth Advisor

As thousands of advisors have completed the American College's Retirement Income Certified Professional (RICP®) designation, many have asked for expanded instruction from my contribution to the curriculum. The Certified Housing Wealth Advisor Course was developed in response to that request.

It is my signature online course and learning community designed to equip advisors with the words, phrases, language, questions, stories and concepts to create planning opportunities from existing clients, acquire new clients, and generate more income.

> For more information, go to
> www.HousingWealthCertification.com

www.HousingWealth.net

Made in the USA
Middletown, DE
04 April 2023

27846318R00110